OECD Insights

Debate the Issues: Complexity and policy making

This work is published under the responsibility of the Secretary-General of the OECD. The opinions expressed and arguments employed herein do not necessarily reflect the official views of OECD member countries.

This document and any map included herein are without prejudice to the status of or sovereignty over any territory, to the delimitation of international frontiers and boundaries and to the name of any territory, city or area.

Please cite this publication as:
OECD (2017), *Debate the Issues: Complexity and policy making*, OECD Insights, OECD Publishing, Paris, *http://dx.doi.org/10.1787/9789264271531-en*.

ISBN 978-92-64-27152-4 (print)
ISBN 978-92-64-27153-1 (PDF)
ISBN 978-92-64-27158-6 (epub)

Series: OECD Insights
ISSN 1993-6745 (print)
ISSN 1993-6753 (online)

Foreword

by
Gabriela Ramos, OECD Chief of Staff and Sherpa to the G20

The OECD has prided itself on its essential role in reconciling the economy with nature and society. At present, the global community is failing to fully grasp and advance this fundamental agenda. To do so we need to improve our analytical frameworks, policy tools and models.

The Financial Crisis, almost ten years ago, was a wake-up call on the inadequacies of our policy approaches. But a number of other important trends were also moving in the wrong direction. Perhaps the most serious indictment of our economic approaches has been the emergence and failure of the international community to take serious action on climate change. A related problem is the unsustainable consumption of the Earth's resources, currently running at 1.6 planets, i.e. it takes the Earth 1 year and 6 months to regenerate what we use in a year.

Inequality in many OECD countries has also been rising steadily and has now reached critical levels, weakening social cohesion and trust while undermining growth and well-being. The boundless pursuit of increased growth and consumption, the traditional treatment of environmental degradation and income inequality as externalities or marginal market failures and the contention that individuals left to their own devices will self-organise into a socially desirable state have been part of the problem. Simply improving the way markets operate will not solve our pressing problems. Alan Kirman argues that the current paradigm is neither validated by empirical evidence nor does it have sound theoretical foundations.

Economists and policy makers have failed to appreciate the complexity of human behaviour and the systems in which we live. A complexity approach allows us to look at systems of systems consisting of vast numbers of individual elements that interact in complicated ways, such as ecosystems, financial markets, and energy networks, or societal phenomena such as urbanisation and migration.

It also challenges mainstream thinking on key issues. For example, according to the Kuznets' curve, income inequality should first rise and then fall as countries' income moves from low to high. The empirical evidence however does not seem to bear this out. In this volume, an approach based on economic complexity by César Hidalgo and others suggests that inequality depends not only on a country's rate or stage of growth, but also on its type of growth and institutions.

In economics, we still talk about flows, masses, equilibrium and so on (a gravity model of trade, for example). But these terms are rooted in classical physics, developed before relativity and quantum theory. The new sciences of complexity can provide insights into how groups of people actually behave when they (re)act together to form economic and socio-political systems. These systems do not operate simply as a series of actions and reactions, but with feedback, non-linearity, tipping points, singularities, emergence, and all the other characteristics of complex systems.

Inspired by the OECD's New Approaches to Economic Challenges (NAEC) initiative, this book *Debate the Issues: Complexity and policy making* provides details of new frameworks that better capture the complexities of modern economies and societies. Our economies are not closed general equilibrium systems; they are complex and adaptive, embedded in specific societies with their own history, culture, and values, as well as in natural environments governed by biophysical laws.

A number of prominent economists have joined this call for a new approach to policy making. Andy Haldane, Chief Economist of the Bank of England writes that NAEC and OECD's willingness to consider a complexity approach "puts the Organisation at the forefront of bringing economic analysis and policy-making into the 21st century". While Eric Beinhocker from the Institute for New Economic Thinking expresses the hope that "the OECD will continue to play a leadership role, through NAEC and its other initiatives, on new economic thinking, not just in a narrow technical sense, but in the broad sense of helping forge a new vision that puts people back at the centre of our economy". While Eric Beinhocker from the Institute for New Economic Thinking expresses the hope that the OECD will continue to play a leadership role, through NAEC and its other initiatives, on new economic thinking, not just in a narrow technical sense, but in the broad sense of helping forge a new vision that puts people back at the centre of our economy.

Having led the NAEC and Inclusive Growth initiatives, I have been pushing the idea at the OECD, in member Countries and Key Partner countries, as well as the G20, that economic growth is a means to an end – not an end in itself. This Insights book argues that our efforts to understand economic growth as a means to improve well-being could benefit from an approach that sees inclusive growth as the outcome of complex interactions among economics, politics, psychology, culture, history, environment, and ambition.

If we want growth to be inclusive, our way of thinking about it has to be inclusive too.

Table of contents

Introduction:
A complexity approach
to economic challenges

by
William Hynes, OECD New Approaches
to Economic Challenges (NAEC) initiative

The OECD launched its New Approaches to Economic Challenges (NAEC) initiative in 2012 to reflect on the lessons for economic analysis and policy making from the financial crisis and Great Recession. European Central Bank Governor Jean-Claude Trichet said that: "As a policy-maker during the crisis, I found the available models of limited help. In fact, I would go further: in the face of the crisis, we felt abandoned by conventional tools". But even before the crisis Greg Mankiw from Harvard University lamented that "macroeconomic research of the past three decades has had only minor impact on the practical analysis of monetary or fiscal policy".

NAEC examined the shortcomings of analytical models, and it promotes new policy tools and data. It questions traditional ideas and methods and challenges group-think and silo approaches by inviting comment and criticism from outside the Organisation, and by soliciting input from social sciences such as sociology, psychology, and history to enrich the policy discussions.

While the financial crisis struck at the core of traditional economic theory and models, it became apparent in 2016 that the failure of economic thinking and acting was far deeper and more destabilising than we thought, so part of NAEC's mandate is to develop an agenda for inclusive and sustainable growth.

This is all the more urgent given the backlash against globalisation, increased inequalities of income and opportunities, and the negative impact of growth on the environment. We need to develop what Eric Beinhocker calls a "new narrative of growth", one that puts people at the centre of economic policy. Therefore NAEC is helping to focus on redistribution, a concept neglected in economic analysis for many years, and helping to ensure that policy decisions improve the lives of those at the bottom of the income distribution.

It is also helping to consider the well-being of people as a multi-dimensional concept, which implies reconsidering important elements of the economic narrative, such as justice and social cohesion. NAEC does so by thinking out of the box, emphasising the need to empower people, regions and firms to fulfil their full potential. This is at the core of the *Productivity-Inclusiveness Nexus* that considers how to expand the productive assets of an economy by investing in the skills of its people; and that provides a level playing field for firms to compete, including in lagging regions.

However, the challenges are too complex and interconnected for conventional models and analyses. As Andy Haldane argues, the global economy is increasingly characterised by discontinuities, tipping points, multiple equilibria, radical uncertainties and the other characteristics of complex systems. This is why a key theme of NAEC has been the complexity and interconnectedness of the economy, exemplified by the *Productivity-Inclusiveness Nexus*.

The contributors to this series argue that complexity and systems thinking can improve understanding of issues such as financial crises, sustainability of growth, competitiveness, innovation, and urban planning. Recognising the complexity of the economy implies that greater attention should be paid to interactions, unintended consequences, stability, resilience, policy buffers and safeguards.

Working with the European Commission and the Institute for New Economic Thinking (INET) Oxford, the NAEC initiative demonstrated in a number of workshops that complexity economics is a promising approach for delivering new insights into major public policy challenges and an exciting research agenda going forward.

The workshops offered a timely opportunity for policy makers, academics and researchers to discuss the policy applications emerging from the study of complexity. The NAEC Roundtable in December 2016 discussed whether economics was close to a tipping point – a transition to a new behavioural complexity paradigm. There is wide agreement among economists on the limitations and the shortcomings of the rational expectations paradigm and much discussion on how to move forward.

The first phase of NAEC's complexity work has made the case for further and deeper examination of complexity. Going forward, it will be important to demonstrate the value of complexity, systems thinking and agent-based models in a number of areas including financial networks, urban systems and the other issues highlighted in this series. The challenge is to demonstrate the value of the approach.

Complexity offers an opportunity for addressing long-held concerns about economic assumptions, theories and models. For the OECD, it also holds out the potential for creating better policies for better lives.

Useful links

The original article on OECD Insights, including links and supplementary material, can be found here: *http://wp.me/p2v6oD-2Pl*

The full series can be found here: *http://oecdinsights.org/?s=NAEC+complexity*

Complexity
and policy making

Stop pretending that an economy can be controlled

by Angel Gurría, OECD Secretary-General

The crisis exposed some serious flaws in our economic thinking. It has highlighted the need to look at economic policy with more critical, fresh approaches. It has also revealed the limitations of existing tools for structural analysis in factoring in key linkages, feedbacks and trade-offs – for example between growth, inequality and the environment.

We should seize the opportunity to develop a new understanding of the economy as a highly complex system that, like any complex system, is constantly reconfiguring itself in response to multiple inputs and influences, often with unforeseen or undesirable consequences. This has many implications. It suggests policy makers should be constantly vigilant and more humble about their policy prescriptions, act more like navigators than mechanics, and be open to systemic risks, spillovers, strengths, weaknesses, and human sensitivities. This demands a change in our mind-sets, and in our textbooks. As John Kenneth Galbraith once said, "the conventional view serves to protect us from the painful job of thinking."

This is why at the OECD we launched an initiative called New Approaches to Economic Challenges (NAEC). With this initiative we want to understand better how the economy works, in all its complexity, and design policies that reflect this understanding. Our aim is to consider and address the unintended consequences of policies, while developing new approaches that foster more sustainable and inclusive growth.

Complexity is a common feature of a growing number of policy issues in an increasingly globalised world employing sophisticated technologies and running against resource constraints.

The report of the OECD Global Science Forum (2009) on Applications of Complexity Science for Public Policy reminds us of the distinction between complicated and complex systems. Traditional science (and technology) excels at the complicated, but is still at an early stage in its understanding of complex phenomena like the climate.

For example, the complicated car can be well understood using normal engineering analyses. An ensemble of cars travelling down a highway, by contrast, is a complex system. Drivers interact and mutually adjust their behaviours based on diverse factors such as perceptions, expectations, habits, even emotions. To understand traffic, and to build better highways, set speed limits, install automatic radar systems, etc., it is helpful to have tools that can accommodate non-linear and collective patterns of behaviour, and varieties of driver types or rules that might be imposed. The tools of complexity science are needed in this case. And we need better rules of the road in a number of areas.

This is not an academic debate. The importance of complexity is not limited to the realm of academia. It has some powerful advocates in the world of policy. Andy Haldane at the Bank of England has thought of the global financial system as a complex system and focused on applying the lessons from other network disciplines – such as ecology, epidemiology, and engineering – to the financial sphere. More generally, it is clear that the language of complexity theory – tipping points, feedback, discontinuities, fat tails – has entered the financial and regulatory lexicon. Haldane has shown the value of adopting a complexity lens, providing insights on structural vulnerabilities that built up in the financial system. This has led to policy suggestions for improving the robustness of the financial system.

Closer to home, Bill White, Chairman of our Economic and Development Review Committee (EDRC) has been an ardent advocate of thinking about the economy as a complex system. He has spoken in numerous OECD meetings – in part as an explanation and in part as a warning – that systems build up as a result of cumulative processes, can have highly unpredictable dynamics and can demonstrate significant non-linearity. As a result Bill has urged policy makers to accept more uncertainty and be more prudent. He also urged economists to learn some exceedingly simple but important lessons from those that have studied or work with complex systems such as biologists, botanists, anthropologists, traffic controllers, and military strategists.

Perhaps the most important insight of complexity is that policy makers should stop pretending that an economy can be controlled. Systems are prone to surprising, large-scale, seemingly uncontrollable, behaviours. Rather, a greater emphasis should be placed on building resilience, strengthening policy buffers and promoting adaptability by fostering a culture of policy experimentation.

At the OECD, we are starting to embrace complexity. For several years we have been mapping the trade "genome" with our Trade in Value Added (TiVA) database to explain the commercial interconnections between countries.

We have examined the possibilities for coupling economic and other systems models, for example environmental (climate) and societal (inequalities). Our work on the Costs of Inaction and Resource Constraints: Implications for Long-term Growth (CIRCLE) is a key example of linking bio-physical models and economic models to gauge the impact of environmental degradation and climate change on the economy.

We are also looking at governing complex systems in areas as diverse as education and international trade policy. And we are looking at the potential for tapping Big Data – an indispensable element of complexity modelling approaches. But there remains much to do to fully enrich our work with the perspectives of complexity.

The OECD is delighted to work with strong partners – the Institute for New Economic Thinking (INET) Oxford, and the European Commission to help policy makers advance the use of complex systems thinking to address some of the most difficult challenges.

An important question remains. How can the insights and methods of complexity science be applied to assist policy makers as they tackle difficult problems in areas such as environmental protection, financial regulation, sustainability or urban development?

The Workshop on Complexity and Policy in September 2016 at the OECD helped find the answer – stimulate new thinking, new policy approaches and ultimately better policies for better lives.

Useful links

The original article on OECD Insights, including links and supplementary material, can be found here: *http://wp.me/p2v6oD-2Dz*

The full series can be found here: *http://oecdinsights.org/?s=NAEC+complexity*

It's not just the economy: Society is a complex system too

by Gabriela Ramos, OECD Chief of Staff and Sherpa to the G20

Income and wealth inequality is not a new phenomenon. On the contrary, it seems that it is a permanent feature in human history, and over the years, its causes and consequences have become more numerous and more interconnected. The same is true for many social phenomena, and even though the world looks more complicated today, it is not. What is different is the increased number of domains where public policy is expected to play a role. Regarding inequalities of income and wealth, governments have to make decisions on several interlinked areas such as taxes, education or health.

Unfortunately, the tools at the disposal of policy makers have not always been updated fast enough to cope with these challenges and with their interlinkages. Moreover, policies are often designed within the narrow confines of one issue, without taking into account their consequences elsewhere.

Economists have tried to simplify and abstract from reality with limiting assumptions like the representative agent and general equilibrium. They have also given primacy to the goal of effectiveness, in detriment to other important considerations such as fairness. Yet, the use of aggregate data obscures the distributional consequences of policies: an economy as a whole may be doing well, but – as we have seen in recent years – there are severe consequences for social cohesion, and ultimately growth itself, if large groups are excluded from the benefits of economic prosperity. In defining growth policies that aimed only at increasing GDP per capita, inadequate attention was paid to institutions, human behaviour, and culture. These approaches failed to adequately account for the realities of markets, consumer decisions, and the interconnectedness of economic, communications and societal networks.

In stark contrast to the assumptions of neo-classical economics, socio-economic systems are not stable, but in constant flux. Complexity science generates new insights and furnishes us with the analytical tools and instruments to help us, as individuals and societies, to navigate this new understanding of the economy. It addresses some of the limitations which constrain conventional economics and ultimately it is helping us to do a better job in advising governments and public institutions.

For example, taking a complexity-based approach we can begin to recognise that the causes and consequences of inequalities and major economic and societal problems are intertwined. Besides contributing substantially to the increase of wealth inequality, the financialisation of the economy also led to increased systemic risks where a problem in the subprime markets led to a major economic crisis that has set additional hurdles in the way of the most vulnerable groups all over the world.

Just like the financial system and its major risks, our social systems are complex and vulnerable. Considering the increased fragmentation and divisions in our societies (and adding the challenge of integration of migrants and marginalised groups) more attention should be paid to social stability. In this vein, policies to address societal problems, should not only rely on traditional economic tools and measures, but broaden them to bring insights of useful disciplines.

This more realistic approach to how people and the economy actually work is needed – an integrated inclusive growth agenda which also considers unintended consequences, trade-offs and complementarities between policy objectives.

Indeed, I believe that economists – and the policy makers they advise – can do better by listening to and learning from others. It's not easy for an organisation that has "Economic" in it is name, but we need to break the monopoly of economics over policy – looking to other disciplines such as physics, biology, psychology, sociology, philosophy and history. Societies and economies are not static features that can be predicted, but evolutionary systems with breakpoints and changes that need to be better characterised.

At the OECD, we recognise the potential of new economic thinking, drawing on complexity theory, and evolutionary and behavioural economics. Technological and analytical innovations are driving a revolution in the physical sciences, biological sciences, and social sciences, breaking down the barriers between disciplines and stimulating new, integrated approaches to pressing and complex challenges. Advances in computing power are opening up new possibilities for integrating systems models, agent-based modelling and network analysis. It is only by properly utilising these new approaches that we can strive to create social and economic models that provide a more accurate representation of the world around us. These tools also allow us to get away from average representations, or to look at stocks and not only at flows in the economy (income vs wealth inequality).

And indeed, economics is starting to incorporate insights from other disciplines. For example, expectations may be admirably rational in traditional models, but by combining psychology and economics we are designing policies based on how real people actually behave, not on limited assumptions about how some fictional average person should behave. Taking a problem-based approach, we can design policies to influence people and nudge them in the right direction in areas such as consumer policy, regulation, and environmental protection.

The OECD is part of this revolution and we are already transforming our policy thinking and acting. With the New Approaches to Economic Challenges (NAEC) initiative, we are taking a hard look at our analytical methods, our data and policy advice.

Many articles in this series have argued that the economy is a complex adaptive system. Society is a complex system too. It is formed by the interaction and mutual dependence of individuals, and is pursuant to their spontaneous, natural behaviour. Since the emergence of hunter-gather societies inequalities have threatened to undermine and weaken the fabric of the social system. If we are to overcome the pernicious effects of these inequalities, we need to think about the interactions between our social and economic systems – which follow their own logics –

and design policies which help our economies to grow. But growth isn't an end in itself. It has to be inclusive to ensure that all segments of our societies prosper.

Systems thinking can lend us a hand to fight inequalities and develop an agenda for inclusive growth. As we draw out the interlinkages between different policy areas, we begin to understand how the economic system interacts with other systems, as well as with the history, politics, and ambitions of countries. Our task now is to put this growing comprehension to good use, in order to make the economy work better for all people.

Useful links

The original article on OECD Insights, including links and supplementary material, can be found here: *http://wp.me/p2v6oD-2DD*

The full series can be found here: *http://oecdinsights.org/?s=NAEC+complexity*

A new role for science in policy formation in the age of complexity?

by Vladimir Šucha, Director General, European Commission, Joint Research Centre

The recent financial crisis was a wakeup call for both scientists and policy makers. It exposed new and unknown links between economic magnitudes but also between various parts of our modern, globalised world. It further helped to reveal the limitations of some approaches in economics as well as social sciences which proved to be unsuitable for this new world.

The crisis, above all, showed that the economy is a highly complex, dynamic and evolving undertaking, with the potential, at times, to produce unpredictable (and often undesired) outcomes. Finally, it showed the need to embrace more appropriately this complexity in the science underlying policy analysis as well as in the policy-making process itself.

So, eight years on from the beginning of the crisis, have scientists and policy makers moved out of their comfort zone? Are new ways of thinking being embraced? Are they being applied in practice? What do we have to do to ensure that they result in better policies and, ultimately, fairer and more resilient societies?

As the European Commission's science and knowledge service, the Joint Research Centre (JRC) is supposed to bridge the gap between science and policy makers, as is the OECD. Based on our experience, we believe that a good deal of progress has been made. However, there is still a lot of work to do if the science dealing with such complexity is to deliver its full potential.

Complexity science, of course, has been around for some decades now. It is the scientific study of complex systems, where many components interact producing a global conduct that could not easily be predicted using simple models only which are based on the ordinary interaction between the individual constituent elements of such systems. Since such systems can be found in many areas of life, complexity science is used in a number of different fields, including biology, social sciences, computer science, transport, energy and critical infrastructure protection.

It has developed quickly in the last few decades. Concepts such as non-linearity, self-adaptation, emergence, chaotic dynamics and multiple equilibria, are now firmly established. Valuable tools have been developed, such as sensitivity analysis, scenario modelling and foresighting, network science and dynamic systems modelling, which allow these concepts to be applied appropriately.

Economics was relatively late to embrace these concepts and tools. However, following the crisis, there is an increased interest in applying them, particularly to financial markets.

The JRC is moving in this direction. For example, our researchers employ network science to estimate interlinkages between the banking sector and other institutional investors and how shocks could propagate within the system.

However, our impression is that, in spite of the stronger interest in recent years, complexity economics still needs to spread more widely among economists. It should not be the preserve of a small number of outsiders only.

We also feel that it is still not as useful as it could be for policy making. This is because it remains rather abstract. In many cases, it can help us to understand the theoretical characteristics or basis of a phenomenon but it is still difficult to use it for practical problem solving. This may either be because the related models are not sufficiently detailed or because the data used are not sufficiently adequate for the problem under consideration.

There are, of course, many novel sources of data available. The task is to develop innovative paradigms for their collection, and also new methods for their analysis, since large amounts of data can often obscure rather than clarify an issue if the appropriate techniques for interpreting and making sense of them are not available.

Scientists, therefore, need to develop new approaches for gathering and organising data, such as how to deal with Big Data or else text and data mining. They also need to explore models and tools for data analysis in a policy context, including indicators, innovative visualisations and impact evaluation methods.

The good news is that policy makers are now opening up, at least to some extent. Most of them now realise that attention to the interlinkages between policy areas and the related objectives, and improving evidence on the simultaneous movement of various targets and policy levers, is essential.

They know that the impact of regulation cannot be judged only on the basis of its specific achievements inside a given context but that it may also produce unintended (and undesired) consequences in other areas outside the context under consideration. There is therefore a potential demand for the greater use of complexity science to understand such wider linkages in complex systems.

However, it can be difficult to explain counter-intuitive results to politicians and policy makers.

Equally, while scientists must make policy makers aware of the complexity of the systems they are dealing with, it is important not to overburden them. If they feel that these systems are so complex that no one can possibly understand or influence them, the result will be inertia and defeatism.

Moreover, there is little point in using complexity science to understand the linkages in systems, unless policy makers are prepared to strive for integrated solutions working with one another, across silos. All are committed to doing this in theory but it does not always happen in practice. DG JRC sees part of its role as organising forums on complex issues, where policy makers from different fields can meet, along with scientists from different disciplines.

It is also important to involve those stakeholders most affected by the phenomena under review. DG JRC is experimenting with new ways of directly involving stakeholders in the "co-design" of public interventions. This is all part of developing a multi-faceted perspective.

Finally, there is a job to do in helping policy makers and politicians to develop simple messages to persuade the public of the merits of the solutions arrived at using complex science.

These are only some very basic reflections on why DG JRC welcomes this event. We are keen to further extend our co-operation with the OECD and the Institute for New Economic Thinking in the area of Complexity and Policy. By co-operating more closely, we believe that we can further improve the role of science in policy formation in our current world of ever increasing complexity.

Useful links

The original article on OECD Insights, including links and supplementary material, can be found here: *http://wp.me/p2v6oD-2Dn*

The full series can be found here: *http://oecdinsights.org/?s=NAEC+complexity*

Ants, algorithms and complexity without management

by Deborah M. Gordon, Department of Biology, Stanford University

Systems without central control are ubiquitous in nature. The activities of brains, such as thinking, remembering and speaking, are the outcome of countless electrical interactions among cells. Nothing in the brain tells the rest of it to think or remember. I study ants because I am interested in how collective outcomes arise from interactions among individuals, and how collective behaviour is tuned to changing environments.

There are more than 14 000 species of ants, which all live in colonies consisting of one or more reproductive females, and many sterile workers, which are the ants that you see walking around. Although the reproductive females are called "queens", they have no power or political authority. One ant never directs the behaviour of another or tells it what to do. Ant colonies manage to collect food, build and maintain nests, rear the young, and deal with neighbouring colonies – all without a plan.

The collective behaviour of colonies is produced by a dynamical network of simple interactions among ants. In most ant species, the ants can barely see. They operate mostly by smell. As an ant moves around it briefly contacts other ants with its antennae, or it may contact a short-lived patch of a volatile chemical recently left behind by another ant. Ants smell with their antennae, and when one ant touches another with its antennae, it assesses whether the other ant is a nestmate, and sometimes what task the other ant has been performing. The ant uses its recent experience of chemical interactions to decide what to do next. In the aggregate, these simple interactions create a constantly shifting network that regulates the behaviour of the colony.

The process that generates simple interactions from colony behaviour is what computer scientists call a distributed algorithm. No single unit, such as an ant or a router in a data network, knows what all the others are doing and tells them what to do. Instead, interactions between each unit and its local connections add up to the desired outcome.

The distributed processes that regulate the collective behaviour of ants are tuned to environmental conditions. For example, harvester ants in the desert face high operating costs, and their behaviour is regulated by feedback that limits activity unless it is necessary. A colony must spend water to get water. The ants get water by metabolising the fats in the seeds they eat. A forager out in the desert sun loses water while out searching for food. Colonies manage this trade-off by a simple form of feedback. An outgoing forager does not leave the nest until it meets enough returning foragers with seeds. This makes sense because each forager searches until it finds food. Thus the more food is available, the more quickly they find it and return to the nest, stimulating more foragers to go out to search. When food is not available, foraging activity decreases. A long-term study of a population of colonies shows that the colonies that conserve water in dry conditions by staying inside are more successful in producing offspring colonies.

By contrast, another species called "turtle ants", living in the trees of a tropical forest in Mexico, regulate their behaviour very differently. The turtle ants create a highway system of trails that links different nests and food sources. Operating costs are low because it is humid in the tropical forest, but competition from other species is high. These ants interact using trail pheromones, laying down a chemical trail everywhere they go. An ant tends to follow another and this simple interaction keeps the stream of ants going, except when it is deterred by encounters with other species. In conditions of low operating costs, interactions create feedback that makes ongoing activity the default state, and uses negative feedback to inhibit activity. Thus this is the opposite of the system for desert ants that require positive feedback to initiate activity.

What can we learn from ants about human society? Ants have been used throughout history as examples of obedience and industry. In Greek mythology, Zeus changes the ants of Thessaly into men, creating an army of soldiers, who would become famous as the Myrmidons ready to die for Achilles (from myrmex – μ μ – ant). In the Bible (Proverbs 4:4), we are told to "Look to the ant" who harvests grain in the summer to save for the winter. But ants are not acting out of obedience, and they are not especially industrious; in fact, many ants just hang around in the nest doing nothing.

Ants and humans are very different. Power and identity are crucial to human social behaviour, and absent in ants. Ants do not have relations with other ants as individuals. As an ant assesses its recent interactions with others, it does not matter whether it met ant number 522 or ant number 677. Even more fundamental, an ant does not act in response to any assessment of what needs to be done.

However, we may be able to learn from ants about the behaviour of very large dynamical networks by focussing on the pattern or structure of interactions rather than the content. While we care about what our emails say, the ants care only about how often they get them. It is clear that many human social processes operate without central control. For instance, we see all around us the effects of climate change driven by many different social processes that are based on the use of fossil fuel. No central authority decided to pump carbon into the atmosphere, but the CO_2 levels are the result of human activity. Another obvious example is the internet, a huge dynamical network of local interactions in the form of email messages and visits to websites. The role of social media in the recent US election reflects how the gap between different networks can produce completely disparate views of what is happening and why.

The most useful insights may come from considering how the dynamics of distributed algorithms evolve in relation to changing conditions. The correspondences between the regulation of collective behaviour and the changing conditions in which it operates might provide insight, and even inspire thinking about policy, in human social systems. For ants or neurons, the network has no content. Studying natural systems can show us how the rhythm of local interactions creates patterns in the behaviour and development of large groups, and how such feedback evolves in response to a changing world.

Useful links

The original article on OECD Insights, including links and supplementary material, can be found here: *http://wp.me/p2v6oD-2JK*

The full series can be found here: *http://oecdinsights.org/?s=NAEC+complexity*

Navigating wicked problems

by Julia Stockdale-Otárola,
OECD Public Affairs and Communications Directorate

Knowing there is a single clear solution to any problem is certainly a comforting idea. As children we would raise our hands in class to answer increasingly difficult questions – always hoping that we would "get it right". But sometimes the question itself is ambiguous and the list of potential solutions endless.

Such is the case with wicked problems.

The term isn't a moral judgement. Wicked problems are dynamic, poorly structured, persistent and social in nature. Difficult to define, highly intertwined with other social issues, and involving many actors, wicked problems reflect the complexity of the world we live in. For example, think of policy challenges such as climate change, immigration, poverty, nutrition, education, or homelessness. Each issue involves multiple drivers, impacting various policy domains and levels of government. To further complicate matters, any intervention could set off a chain of new unintended consequences. That's a lot of moving parts.

All these factors make it difficult for anyone to agree on what the actual problem is, where it is rooted, who is responsible, and how to best address it. The scope of the problem is also vague. Entire systems can be involved in a seemingly local or regional problem like mass transit.

Clearly coming to grips with the issue is challenge enough, so how do we go about making decisions? So far, traditional approaches have proven unsatisfactory. In fact, many of these wicked problems seem to only get worse as we try to solve them.

The complexities involved force us to rethink our problem-solving strategy. Instead of trying to find a final solution we need to recognise that these challenges can, generally speaking, at best be managed but not solved. At least, not solved in a static sense. That doesn't mean the situation can't be improved. To some, it might even be "solved" depending on how the problem is defined. The bottom line is that we need to become more flexible to better manage the challenges posed by wicked problems. Policies should be adaptive, so that they can change as the issue evolves over time. We also need to avoid becoming too attached to our own solutions. They need to be dynamic, to change along with the problem at hand.

From the outset we need to look at problems more holistically. An increasing number of new approaches are developing in different fields to offer solutions. Complexity science is naturally adaptive as it looks at the way in which systems interact. To date this strategy has been helpful for example in improving traffic management. To improve traffic safety analytics techniques are applied to anticipate risks and traffic jams, and improve flow. Implementing pilot projects can also be useful in addressing wicked problems, when affordable, as they involve continuous monitoring and opportunity for adjustments. Though no magic formula exists, these approaches can help capture some of the intricacies of wicked problems.

Governments have already started using some of these adaptive strategies. Singapore's government has introduced a mix of policy approaches to tackle wicked problems. For example, a matrix approach was implemented to help departments better share information and work horizontally; new departments reflecting the thorniest issues were established; and a computerised tool to help mitigate systemic risks was introduced. Though the island has the advantage of size, facilitating the implementation of new approaches, their experiences may provide some useful insights into best practices.

The OECD has also been looking at policy challenges as wicked problems. In a 2009 workshop on policy responses to societal concerns, Sandra Batie and David Schweikhardt of Michigan State University analysed trade liberalisation as a wicked problem. In this case, the role of stakeholders is typical of a wicked problem: different groups are likely to have differing ideas about what the real problem is and what its causes are. Some would say the issue is making the economy as open as possible while for others national sovereignty or protecting local producers may be more important.

Unlike a tame problem where scientifically based protocols guide the choice of solution, answers to the question of whether more trade liberalisation is needed depend on the judgements and values of whoever is answering. Many stakeholders will simply reject outright arguments to justify trade liberalisation based on neoclassical economics. Batie and Schweikhardt argued that the role of science, including economic science, is not to narrow the range of options to one (in this case trade liberalisation), but rather to expand the options for addressing the issue(s), and to highlight the consequences, including distributional consequences, of alternative options.

Wicked problems remind us that it isn't always easy, or even possible, to "get it right". There isn't always a solution that can be implemented once and last forever. But that's okay. We just need to stop thinking about achieving optimal solutions and learn how to sustain adaptive solutions.

Useful links

The original article on OECD Insights, including links and supplementary material, can be found here: *http://wp.me/p2v6oD-2DR*

The full series can be found here: *http://oecdinsights.org/?s=NAEC+complexity*

Out of complexity, a third way?

by Bill Below, OECD Directorate for Public Governance
and Territorial Development

The perennial curmudgeon H.L. Mencken is famously misquoted as saying: "For every complex problem there is an answer that is clear, simple, and wrong." The ability to simplify is of course one of our strengths as humans. As a species, we might just as well have been called homo redactor – after all, to think is to find patterns and organise complexity, to reduce it to actionable options or spin it into purposeful things. Behavioural economists have identified a multitude of short-cuts we use to reduce complex situations into actionable information. These hard-wired tricks, or heuristics, allow us to make decisions on the fly, providing quick answers to questions such as 'should I trust you?', or 'Is it better to cash in now, or hold out for more later?' Are these tricks reliable? Not always. A little due diligence never hurts when listening to one's gut instincts, and the value of identifying heuristics is in part to understand the limits of their usefulness and the potential blind spots they create. The point is, there is no shortage of solutions to problems, whether we generate them ourselves or receive them from experts. And there's no dearth of action plans and policies built on them. So, the issue isn't so much how do we find answers? – We seem to have little trouble doing that. The real question is, how do we get to the right answers, particularly in the face of unrelenting complexity?

There's a nomenclature in the hierarchy of complexity as well as proper and improper ways of going about problem solving at each level. This is presented in the new publication *From Transactional to Strategic: Systems Approaches to Public Challenges* (OECD, 2017), a survey of strategic systems thinking in the public sector. Developed by IBM in the 2000s, the Cynefin Framework posits four levels of systems complexity: obvious, complicated, complex and chaotic. Obvious challenges imply obvious answers. But the next two levels are less obvious. While we tend to use the adjectives 'complicated' and 'complex' interchangeably in casual conversation, the framework imposes a formal distinction. Complicated systems/issues have at least one answer and are characterised by causal relationships (although sometimes hidden at first). Complex systems are in constant flux. In complicated systems, we know what we don't know (known unknowns) and apply our expertise to fill in the gaps. In complex systems, we don't know what we don't know (unknown unknowns) and cause and effect relations can only be deduced after the fact. That doesn't mean one can't make inroads into understanding and even shaping a complex system, but you need to use methods adapted to the challenge. A common bias is to mistake complexity for mere complication. The result is overconfidence that a solution is just around the corner and the wrong choice of tools.

Unfortunately, mismatches between organisational structures and problem structures are common. Institutions have specific and sometimes rather narrow remits and often act without a broader vision of what other institutions are doing or planning. Each institution may have its specific expertise yet few opportunities for sustained, trans-agency approaches to solving complex issues.

Thus, top-down, command-and-control institutional structures breed their own resistance to the kind of holistic, whole-of-government approach that complex problems and systems thinking require. This may be an artefact of the need for structures that adapt efficiently to new mandates in the form of political appointees overseeing a stable core of professional civil servants. Also, the presence of elected or appointed officials at the top of clearly defined government institutions may be emblematic of the will of the people being heard. Structural resistance may also stem from competitive political cycles, discouraging candidates to engage in cycle-spanning, intertemporal trade-offs or commit to projects with complex milestones. In a world of sound-bites, fake news and scorched earth tactics, a reasoned, methodical and open-ended systems approach can be a large, slow-moving political target.

And that's the challenge of approaching complex, 'wicked' problems with the appropriate institutional support and scale – there must be fewer sweeping revolutions or cries of total failure by the opposition. Disruption gives way to continuous progress as the complex system evolves from within. It is a kind of third way that eschews polarisation and favours collaboration, that blends market principles with what might be called 'state guidance' rather than top-down intervention.

Global warming, policies for ageing populations, child protection services and transportation management are all examples of complex systems and challenges. Complex systems are hard to define at the outset and open ended in scope. They can only be gradually altered, component by component, sub-system by sub-system, by learning from multiple feedback loops, measuring what works and evaluating how much closer it takes you to your goals.

General Systems Theory (GST), that is, thinking about what is characteristic of systems themselves, sprang from a bold new technological era in which individual fields of engineering were no longer sufficient to master the breath taking range of knowledge and skills required by emerging systems integration. That know-how gave us complex entities as fearful as the Intercontinental Ballistic Missile and as inspiring as manned space flight. Today, the world seems to be suffering from complexity fatigue, whose symptoms are a longing for simple answers and a world free of interdependencies, with clear good guys and bad guys and brash, unyielding voices that 'tell it like it is', a world with lines drawn, walls built and borders closed. Bringing back a sense of excitement and purpose in mastering complexity may be the first 'wicked' problem we should tackle.

In the meantime, we need to find a way to stop approaching complex challenges through the limits of our institutions and start approaching them through the contours of the challenges themselves. Otherwise too many important decisions will be clear, simple and wrong.

Useful links

The original article on OECD Insights, including links and supplementary material, can be found here: *http://wp.me/p2v6oD-2Or*

The full series can be found here: *http://oecdinsights.org/?s=NAEC+complexity*

Complexity and economics

Complexity and economic policy

by Alan Kirman, École des hautes études en sciences sociales, Paris, and Aix-Marseille University

Over the last two centuries there has been a growing acceptance of social and political liberalism as the desirable basis for societal organisation. Economic theory has tried to accommodate itself to that position and has developed increasingly sophisticated models to justify the contention that individuals left to their own devices will self-organise into a socially desirable state. However, in so doing, it has led us to a view of the economic system that is at odds with what has been happening in many other disciplines.

Although in fields such as statistical physics, ecology and social psychology it is now widely accepted that systems of interacting individuals will not have the sort of behaviour that corresponds to that of one average or typical particle or individual, this has not had much effect on economics. Whilst those disciplines moved on to study the emergence of non-linear dynamics as a result of the complex interaction between individuals, economists relentlessly insisted on basing their analysis on that of rational optimising individuals behaving as if they were acting in isolation. Indeed, this is the basic paradigm on which modern economic theory and our standard economic models are based. It dates from Adam Smith's (1776) notion of the Invisible Hand which suggested that when individuals are left, insofar as possible, to their own devices, the economy will self-organise into a state which has satisfactory welfare properties.

Yet this paradigm is neither validated by empirical evidence nor does it have sound theoretical foundations. It has become an assumption. It has been the cornerstone of economic theory although the persistent arrival of major economic crises would seem to suggest that there are real problems with the analysis. Experience suggests that amnesia is prevalent among economists and that, while each crisis provokes demands for new approaches to economics, (witness the birth of George Soros' Institute for New Economic Thinking), in the end inertia prevails and economics returns to the path that it was already following.

There has been a remarkable tendency to use a period of relative calm to declare victory over the enemy. Recall the declaration of Robert Lucas, Nobel Prize winner and President of the American Economic Association in his Presidential Address in 2003 in which he said: "The central problem of depression-prevention has been solved."

Both economists and policy makers had been lulled into a sense of false security during this brief period of calm.

Then came 2008 and, as always in times of crisis, voices were raised, mainly by commentators and policy makers enquiring as to why economists had anticipated neither the onset nor the severity of the crisis.

When Her Majesty the Queen asked economists at the London School of Economics what had gone wrong, she received the following reply: "In summary your majesty, the failure to foresee the timing, extent and severity of the crisis … was principally the failure of the collective imagination of many bright people … to understand the risks to the system as a whole."

As soon as one considers the economy as a complex adaptive system in which the aggregate behaviour emerges from the interaction between its components, no simple relation between the individual participant and the aggregate can be established. Because of all the interactions and the complicated feedbacks between the actions of the individuals and the behaviour of the system there will inevitably be "unforeseen consequences" of the actions taken by individuals, firms and governments. Not only the individuals themselves but the network that links them changes over time. The evolution of such systems is intrinsically difficult to predict, and for policy makers this means that assertions such as "this measure will cause that outcome" have to be replaced with "a number of outcomes are possible and our best estimates of the probabilities of those outcomes at the current point are…"

Consider the case of the possible impact of Brexit on the British economy and the global economy. Revised forecasts of the growth of these economies are now being issued, but when so much depends on the conditions under which the exit is achieved, is it reasonable to make such deterministic forecasts? Given the complexity and interlocking nature of the economies, the political factors that will influence the nature of the separation and the perception and anticipation of the participants (from individuals to governments) of the consequences, how much confidence can we put in point estimates of growth over the next few years?

While some might take the complex systems approach as an admission of our incapacity to control or even influence economic outcomes, this need not be the case. Hayek once argued that there are no economic "laws" just "patterns". The development of Big Data and the techniques for its analysis may provide us with the tools to recognise such patterns and to react to them. But these patterns arise from the interaction of individuals who are in many ways simpler than *homo economicus*, and it is the interaction between these relatively simple individuals who react to what is going on, rather than optimise in isolation that produces the major upheavals that characterise our systems.

Finally, in trying to stabilise such systems it is an error to focus on one variable either to control the system or to inform us about its evolution. Single variables such as the interest rate do not permit sufficient flexibility for policy actions and single performance measures such as the unemployment rate or GDP convey too little information about the state of the economy.

Useful links

The original article on OECD Insights, including links and supplementary material, can be found here: *http://wp.me/p2v6oD-2B4*

The full series can be found here: *http://oecdinsights.org/?s=NAEC+complexity*

A pragmatic holist: Herbert Simon, economics and *The Architecture of Complexity*

by Vela Velupillai, Madras School of Economics

> "Herb had it all put together at least 40 years ago – and I've known him only for 35." Alan Newell, 1989.

And so it was, with *Hierarchy* in 1950, *Near-Decomposability* from about 1949, and *Causality,* underpinning the reasonably rapid evolution of dynamical systems into a series of stable complex structures. Almost all of these pioneering articles are reprinted in Simon's 1977 collection and, moreover, the hierarchy and near-decomposability classics appear in section 4 with the heading "Complexity". The cybernetic vision became the fully-fledged digital computer basis of boundedly rational human problem solvers implementing heuristic search procedures to prove, for example, axiomatic mathematical theorems (in the monumental *Principia Mathematica* of Russell and Whitehead) substantiating Alan Newell's entirely reasonable claim quoted above.

In defining the notion of complexity in *The Architecture of Complexity* (AoC), Simon eschews formalisms and relies on a rough, working, concept of complex systems that would help identify examples of observable structures – predominantly in the behavioural sciences – that could lead to theories and, hence, theorems, of evolving dynamical systems that exhibit properties that are amenable to design and prediction with the help of hierarchy, near-decomposability and causality. Thus, the almost informal definition is (italics added): "*Roughly,* by *a complex system* I mean one made up of a large number of parts that interact in a *nonsimple* way. In such systems, the whole is more than the sum of the parts ... in the ... pragmatic sense that, given the properties of the parts and the laws of their interaction, it is not a trivial matter to infer the properties of the whole. In the face of *complexity,* an in-principle reductionist may be at the same time a *pragmatic holist.*"

Simon was always a pragmatic holist, even while attempting the reduction of the behaviour of complex entities to parsimonious processes that would exhibit the properties of "wholes", based on nonsimply interacting "parts", that may themselves be simple. He summarised the way this approach could apply to economics in a letter to Professor Axel Leijonhufvud and me after reading my book *Computable Economics*. (You can see the letter *here*.) Simon argued that:

"Finally, we get to the empirical boundary … of the level of complexity that humans actually can handle, with and without their computers, and – perhaps more important – what they actually do to solve problems that lie beyond this strict boundary even though they are within some of the broader limits.

The latter is an important point for economics, because we humans spend most of our lives making decisions that are far beyond any of the levels of complexity we can handle exactly; and this is where satisficing, floating aspiration levels, recognition and heuristic search, and similar devices for arriving at good-enough decisions take over. [The term 'satisfice', which appears in the *Oxford English Dictionary* as a Northumbrian synonym for 'satisfy', was borrowed by Simon (1956) in 'Rational Choice and the Structure of the Environment' to describe a strategy for reaching a decision the decider finds adequate, even if it's not optimal in theory.] A parsimonious economic theory, and an empirically verifiable one, shows how human beings, using very simple procedures, reach decisions that lie far beyond their capacity for finding exact solutions by the usual maximizing criteria."

In many ways, AoC summarised Simon's evolving (sic!) visions of a quantitative behavioural science, which provided the foundations of administering complex, hierarchically structured, causal organisations, by boundedly rational agents implanting – with the help of digital computers – procedures that were, in turn, reflections of human problem solving processes. But it also presaged the increasing precision of predictable reality – not amounting to non-pragmatic, non-empirical phenomena – requiring an operational description of complex systems that were the observable in nature, resulting from the evolutionary dynamics of hierarchical structures. Thus, the final – fourth – section of AoC "examines the relation between complex systems and their descriptions" – for which Simon returned to Solomonoff's pioneering definition of algorithmic information theory.

AoC was equally expository on the many issues with which we have come to associate Simon's boundedly rational agents (and Institutions) satisficing – instead of optimising, again for pragmatic, historically observable, realistic reasons – using heuristic search processes in Human Problem Solving contexts of behavioural decisions. The famous distinction between substantive and procedural rationality arose from the dichotomy of a state vs process description of a world "as sensed and … as acted upon".

Essentially AoC is suffused with pragmatic definitions and human procedures of realistic implementations, even in the utilising of digital computers. Computability theory assumes the *Church-Turing Thesis* in defining algorithms. The notion of computational complexity is predicated upon the assumption of the validity of the Church-Turing Thesis. Simon's algorithms for human problem solvers are heuristic search processes, where no such assumption is made. Hence the feeling that engulfed him in his later years is not surprising (italics added):

"The field of computer science has been much occupied with questions of *computational complexity*, the obverse of computational simplicity. But in the literature of the field, 'complexity' usually means something quite different from my meaning of it in the present context. Largely for reasons of mathematical attainability, and *at the expense of relevance*, theorems of computational complexity have mainly addressed worst-case behaviour of computational algorithms as the size of the data set grows larger. In the limit, they have even focused on computability in the sense of Gödel, and Turing and the *halting problem*. I must confess that these concerns *produce in me a great feeling of ennui*."

Useful links

The original article on OECD Insights, including links and supplementary material, can be found here: *http://wp.me/p2v6oD-2Lg*

The full series can be found here: *http://oecdinsights.org/?s=NAEC+complexity*

From economic crisis to crisis in economics

by Andy Haldane, Chief Economist and Executive Director,
Monetary Analysis & Statistics, Bank of England

It would be easy to become very depressed at the state of economics in the current environment. Many experts, including economics experts, are simply being ignored. But the economic challenges facing us could not be greater: slowing growth, slowing productivity, the retreat of trade, the retreat of globalisation, high and rising levels of inequality. These are deep and diverse problems facing our societies and we will need deep and diverse frameworks to help understand them and to set policy in response to them. In the pre-crisis environment when things were relatively stable and stationary, our existing frameworks in macroeconomics did a pretty good job of making sense of things.

But the world these days is characterised by features such as discontinuities, tipping points, multiple equilibria, and radical uncertainty. So if we are to make economics interesting and the response to the challenges adequate, we need new frameworks that can capture the complexities of modern societies.

We are seeing increased interest in using complexity theory to make sense of the dynamics of economic and financial systems. For example, epidemiological models have been used to understand and calibrate regulatory capital standards for the largest, most interconnected banks, the so-called "super-spreaders". Less attention has been placed on using complexity theory to understand the overall architecture of public policy – how the various pieces of the policy jigsaw fit together as a whole in relation to modern economic and financial systems. These systems can be characterised as a complex, adaptive "system of systems", a nested set of sub-systems, each one itself a complex web. The architecture of a complex system of systems means that policies with varying degrees of magnification are necessary to understand and to moderate fluctuations. It also means that taking account of interactions between these layers is important when gauging risk.

Although there is no generally-accepted definition of complexity, that proposed by Herbert Simon in *The Architecture of Complexity* – "one made up of a large number of parts that interact in a non-simple way" – captures well its everyday essence. The whole behaves very differently than the sum of its parts. The properties of complex systems typically give rise to irregular, and often highly non-normal, statistical distributions for these systems over time. This manifests itself as much fatter tails than a normal distribution would suggest. In other words, system-wide interactions and feedbacks generate a much higher probability of catastrophic events than Gaussian distributions would imply.

For evolutionary reasons of survival of the fittest, Simon posited that "decomposable" networks were more resilient and hence more likely to proliferate. By decomposable networks, he meant organisational structures which could be partitioned such that the resilience of the system as a whole was not reliant on any one sub-element. This may be a reasonable long-run description of some real-world complex systems, but less suitable as a description of the evolution of socio-economic systems. The efficiency of many of today's networks relies on their hyper-connectivity. There are, in the language of economics, significantly increasing returns to scale and scope in a network industry. Think of the benefits of global supply chains and global interbank networks for trade and financial risk-sharing. This provides a powerful secular incentive for non-decomposable socio-economic systems.

Moreover, if these hyper-connected networks do face systemic threat, they are often able to adapt in ways which avoid extinction. For example, the risk of social, economic or financial disorder will typically lead to an adaptation of policies to prevent systemic collapse. These adaptive policy responses may preserve otherwise-fragile socio-economic topologies. They may even further encourage the growth of connectivity and complexity of these networks. Policies to support "super-spreader" banks in a crisis for instance may encourage them to become larger and more complex. The combination of network economies and policy responses to failure means socio-economic systems may be less Darwinian, and hence decomposable, than natural and biological systems.

What public policy implications follow from this complex system of systems perspective? First, it underscores the importance of accurate data and timely mapping of each layer in the system. This is especially important when these layers are themselves complex. Granular data is needed to capture the interactions within and between these complex sub-systems.

Second, modelling of each of these layers, and their interaction with other layers, is likely to be important, both for understanding system risks and dynamics and for calibrating potential policy responses to them.

Third, in controlling these risks, something akin to the Tinbergen Rule is likely to apply: there is likely to be a need for at least as many policy instruments as there are complex sub-components of a system of systems if risk is to be monitored and managed effectively. Put differently, an under-identified complex system of systems is likely to result in a loss of control, both system-wide and for each of the layers.

In the meantime, there is a crisis in economics. For some, it is a threat. For others it is an opportunity to make a great leap forward, as Keynes did in the 1930s. But seizing this opportunity requires first a re-examination of the contours of economics and an exploration of some new pathways. Second, it is important to look at economic systems through a cross-disciplinary lens. Drawing on insights from a range of disciplines, natural as well as social sciences, can provide a different perspective on individual behaviour and system-wide dynamics.

The New Approaches to Economic Challenges (NAEC) initiative does so, and the OECD's willingness to consider a complexity approach puts the Organisation at the forefront of bringing economic analysis policy making into the 21st century.

This article draws on contributions to the OECD NAEC Roundtable on 14 December 2016; The GLS Shackle Biennial Memorial Lecture on 10 November 2016; and "On microscopes and telescopes", at the Lorentz centre, Leiden, workshop on socio-economic complexity on 27 March 2015.

Useful links

The original article on OECD Insights, including links and supplementary material, can be found here: *http://wp.me/p2v6oD-2M4*

The full series can be found here: *http://oecdinsights.org/?s=NAEC+complexity*

Complexity theory and evolutionary economics

by Robert D. Atkinson, President, Information Technology and Innovation Foundation

If there was any possible upside from the destruction stemming from the financial crisis and Great Recession it was that neoclassical economics' intellectual hegemony began to be more seriously questioned. As such, the rising interest in complexity theory is a welcome development. Indeed, approaching economic policy from a complexity perspective promises significant improvements. However, this will only be the case if we avoid a Hayekian passivity grounded in the view that action is too risky given just how complex economic systems are. This would be a significant mistake for the risk of non-action in complex systems is often higher than the risk of action, especially if the latter is informed by a rigorous thinking grounded in robust argumentation.

The flaws of neoclassical economics have long been pointed out, including its belief of the "economy as machine", where, if policy makers pull a lever they will get an expected result. However, despite what Larry Summers has written, economics is not a science that applies for all times and places. It is a doctrine and as economies evolve so too should doctrines. After the Second World War, when the United States was shifting from what Michael Lind calls the second republic (the post-Civil War governance system) to the third republic (the post-New-Deal, Great Society governance structure), there was an intense intellectual debate about the economic policy path America should take. In *Keynes-Hayek: The Clash That Defined Modern Economics*, Nicholas Wapshott described this debate between Keynes (a proponent of the third republic), who articulated the need for a larger and more interventionist state, and Hayek (a defender of the second republic), who worried about state over-reach. Today, we are in need of a similar great debate about the future of economic policy for the emerging "fourth republic."

If we are to develop such an economic doctrine to guide the current socio-technical economic system, then complexity will need to play a foundational role. But a risk of going down the complexity path is that proponents may substitute one ideology for another. If today's policy makers believe that economic systems are relatively simple and that policies generate only first-order effects, policy makers who have embraced complexity may believe that second, third, and fourth order effects are rampant. In other words, the butterfly in Mexico can set off a tornado in Texas. If things are this complex, we are better off following Hayek's advice to intervene as little as possible. At least with a mechanist view, policy makers felt they could do something and perhaps they got it right. Hayekian complexity risks leading to inaction.

This gets to a second challenge, "group think." Many advocates of complexity point to complex financial tools (such as collateralised debt obligations, CDOs) as the cause of the financial crisis. Regulators simply didn't have any insight because of the complexity of the instruments. But these tools were symptoms. At the heart of crisis, at least in the United States, was mortgage origination fraud. The even more serious problem was intellectual: virtually all neoclassical economists subscribed to the theory that in an efficient market, all the information that would allow an investor to predict the next price move is already reflected in the current price. If housing prices increase 80% in just a few years, then their actual worth increased 80%. So any reset of economics has to be based not just on replacing many of the basic tenants of neoclassical economics, it has to be based on replacing a troubling tendency toward group think. Yet, replacing the former may indeed be harder than the latter.

So where should we go with complexity? I believe that a core component of complexity is and should be evolution. In an evolutionary view, an economy is an "organism" that is constantly developing new industries, technologies, organisations, occupations, and capabilities while at the same time shedding older ones that new technologies and other evolutionary changes make redundant. This rate of evolutionary change differs over time and space, depending on a variety of factors, including technological advancement, entrepreneurial effort, domestic policies, and the international competitive environment. To the extent that neoclassical models consider change, it is seen as growth more than evolution. In other words, market transactions maximise static efficiency and consumer welfare. As Alan Blinder writes, "Can economic activities be rearranged so that some people are made better off, but no one is made worse off? If so we have uncovered an inefficiency. If not, the system is efficient."

In complexity or evolutionary economics, we should be focusing not on static allocative efficiency, but on adaptive efficiency. Douglass North argues that: "Adaptive efficiency … is concerned with the kinds of rules that shape the way an economy evolves through time. It is also concerned with the willingness of a society to acquire knowledge and learning, to induce innovation, to undertake risk and creative activity of all sorts, as well as to resolve problems and bottlenecks of the society through time." Likewise, Richard Nelson and Sidney G. Winter wrote in their 1982 book *An Evolutionary Theory of Economic Change*, "The broader connotations of 'evolutionary' include a concern with processes of long-term and progressive change."

This provides a valuable direction. It means that a key focus for economic policy should be to encourage adaptation, experimentation and risk taking. It means supporting policies to intentionally accelerate economic evolution, especially from technological and institutional innovation. This means not only rejecting neo-Ludditism in favour of techno-optimism, it means the embrace of a proactive innovation policy. And it means enabling new experiments in policy, recognising that many will fail, but that some will succeed and become "dominant species." Policy and programme experimentation will better enable economic policy to support complex adaptive systems.

Useful links

The original article on OECD Insights, including links and supplementary material, can be found here: *http://wp.me/p2v6oD-2Df*

The full series can be found here: *http://oecdinsights.org/?s=NAEC+complexity*

Complexity, modesty and economic policy

by Lex Hoogduin, University of Groningen and GloComNet

Societies and economies are complex systems, but the theories used to inform economic policies predominantly neglect complexity. They assume for example representative agents such as typical consumers, and they also assume that the future is risky rather than uncertain. This assumption allows for the application of the probability calculus and a whole series of other techniques based on it.

In risk situations, all potential outcomes of a policy can be known. This is not the case in situations of uncertainty, but human beings, policy makers included, cannot escape having to take their decisions and having to act facing an uncertain future. The argument is one of logic. Human beings cannot know now what will be discovered in the future. Future discoveries may however impact and shape the consequences of their current decisions and actions. Therefore, they are unable to come up with an exhaustive list of potential outcomes of a policy decision or action.

Properly taking into account the complexity of the economy and the uncertainty of the future implies a paradigm shift in economics. That paradigm does not need to be developed from scratch. It builds on modern complexity science, neo-Austrian economics (in particular Hayek and von Mises), as well as the work of Keynes and Knight and certain strands of cognitive psychology (for example, Kahneman 2011). There is no room here to elaborate on the theory and the claim that it entails a paradigm shift. Rather, I will discuss the implications for economic policy that follow from this paradigm.

This starts with the recognition that the future cannot be predicted in detail. We should be modest about what can be achieved with economic policy. This is the "modesty principle". Economic policy cannot deliver specific targets for economic growth, income distribution, inflation, the increase of the average temperature in four decades from now, etc. Economic policy makers would be wise to stop pretending that they can deliver what they cannot. This insight implies that many current policies should be discontinued. To mention just one example: inflation targeting by central banks does not pass the modesty test.

This principle also implies refraining from detailed economic forecasts as a basis for policy making and execution. Policies should not be made on the assumption that we know the value of certain variables which we cannot know. An example here is the income multiplier in relation to changes in fiscal policy. The modesty principle also flashes red for risk-based regulation and supervision.

What economic policy can do is contribute to the formation and evolution of a fit economic order, and avoid doing harm to such an order, what I would call the "do no harm principle", and be as little as possible a source of uncertainty for private economic agents.

Order is a central concept in the alternative paradigm, replacing the (dis)equilibrium concept in mainstream economics. An order is the set of possible general outcomes (patterns, like growth, inflation, cyclicality, etc.) emerging from purposefully acting and interacting individuals on the basis of a set of rules in a wide sense (laws, ethics, conventions…), together called a regime. Economics can analyse the connection between changes in regime and changes in economic order. Economic policy can influence the economic order through changing the regime.

However, this knowledge is not certain. There is always the potential for surprises (positive and negative; opportunities and threats) and unintended consequences. Policy can therefore not be designed first and then just be executed as designed. Policy making and execution have to evolve in a process of constant monitoring and adaptation. This would also allow for evolutionary change. An economic order that is not allowed to evolve may lose its fitness and may suddenly collapse or enter a crisis (as described by Scheffer for critical transitions in society). This mechanism may have played a role in the Great Moderation leading up to the financial crisis of 2007/2008 and in the crisis of fully funded pension systems. It is also a warning against basing sustainability policies on precise temperature targets decades in the unknowable future.

Fitness of an order has five dimensions. The first is an order in which agents are acting as described in the previous paragraph – policy making involves a process of constant monitoring and adaptation. In addition to that, fitness is determined by alertness of agents (the ability to detect mistakes and opportunities); their resilience (the ability to survive and recover from mistakes and negative surprises); adaptive capacity (the ability to adjust); and creative capacity (the ability to imagine and shape the future). Policies may be directed at facilitating economic agents to improve these capacities, although constrained by the "modesty" and "do no harm" principles. Note that the concept of stability does not appear in the definition of fitness. This marks a difference with current policies which put much emphasis on stability.

In its own actions the government should be transparent and predictable. The best way to do that seems to be to follow simple rules. For example in fiscal policy, balance the budget, perhaps with clearly-defined, limited room for automatic stabilisers to work.

This alternative paradigm places highlights on some methods and analytical techniques, including narrative techniques, network analysis, evolutionary logic, qualitative scenario thinking, non-linear dynamics (Scheffer), historical analysis (development of complex systems is path dependent) and (reverse) stress testing.

Economic policies developed along these lines help people to live their lives as they wish. They are good policies for good lives.

Useful links

The original article on OECD Insights, including links and supplementary material, can be found here: *http://wp.me/p2v6oD-2CF*

The full series can be found here: *http://oecdinsights.org/?s=NAEC+complexity*

The rising complexity of the global economy

by Sony Kapoor, Managing Director, Re-Define International
Think Tank and CEO of Court Jesters Consulting

A complicated system (such as a car) can be disassembled and understood as the sum of its parts. In contrast, a complex system (such as traffic) exhibits emergent characteristics that arise out of the interaction between its constituent parts. Applying complexity theory to economic policy making requires this important recognition – that the economy is not a complicated system, but a complex one.

Historically, economic models and related policy making have treated the economy as a complicated system where simplified and stylised models, often applied to a closed economy, a specific sector or looking only at particular channels of interaction such as interest rates, seek to first simplify the real economy, then understand it and finally generalise in order to make policy.

This approach is increasingly out-dated and will produce results that simply fail to capture the rising complexity of the modern economy. Any policy decisions based on this notion of a complicated system that is the sum of its parts can be dangerously inaccurate and inappropriate. What are the forces driving this increasing complexity in the global economy? What, if anything, can be done about this?

A complex system can be roughly understood as a network of nodes, where the nodes themselves are interconnected to various degrees through single or multiple channels. This means that whatever happens in one node is transmitted through the network and is likely to impact other nodes to various degrees. The behaviour of the system as a whole thus depends on the nodes, as well as the nature of the inter-linkages between them. The complexity of the system, in this instance the global economy, is influenced by a number of factors. These include first, the number of nodes; second, the number of inter-linkages; third, the nature of interlinkages; and fourth, the speed at which a stimulus or shock propagates to other nodes. Let us now apply each of these factors to the global economy.

The global economy has seen a rapid increase in the number of nodes. One way of understanding this is to look at countries that are active participants in the global economy. The growth of China and other emerging markets, as well as their increasing integration into the world trading and more recently global financial systems, is a good proxy to track the rise in the number of nodes. The relative size and importance of these nodes has also risen with the People's Republic of China, by some measures already the world's largest economy.

Simultaneously, the number of interlinkages between nodes has risen even more rapidly. The number of possible connections between nodes increases non-linearly with the increase in the number of nodes, so the global economy now has a greater number of financial, economic, trade, information, policy, institutional, technology, military, travel and human links between nodes than ever before. The increasing complexity of supply chains in trade and manufacturing, ever greater outsourcing of services, rising military collaborations, the global nature of new technological advances, increasing migration and travel, as well the rise of the internet and telecommunications traffic across the world have all greatly increased the number of connections across the nodes.

It is not just that the number of interconnections between nodes has risen almost exponentially. The scope and nature of these interlinkages has broadened significantly. The most notable broadening has come in the form of the rapid rise of complex manufacturing supply chains; financial links that result directly from the gradual dismantling of capital controls; and the rise of cross-border communication and spread of information through the internet. These ever-broadening connections between different nodes fundamentally change the behaviour of the system and how the global economy will react to any stimulus, change or shock in one or more of nodes in ways that become ever harder to model or predict.

Last but not the least, it is not just the number and intensity of links between the nodes that has risen, but also how quickly information, technology, knowledge, shocks, finance or pathogens move between the nodes. This results in complexity theory parlance, in an ever more tightly coupled global economy. Such systems are more efficient, and the quest for efficiency has given rise to just-in-time supply chains and the rising speed of financial trading and other developments. But this efficiency comes at the cost of rising fragility. Evidence that financial, economic, pathogenic, security and other shocks are spreading more rapidly through the world is mounting.

To sum up, the Dynamic Stochastic General Equilibrium (DSGE) models and other traditional approaches to modelling the global economy are increasingly inadequate and inaccurate in capturing the rising complexity of the global economy. This complexity is being driven both by the rising number of nodes (countries) now integrated into the global economy, as well as the number and nature of the interconnections between these, which are intensifying at an even faster pace.

This calls for a new approach to policy making that incorporates lessons from complexity theory by using a system-wide approach to modelling, changes institutional design to reduce the fragility of the system and deepens international and cross-sector policy making and policy co-ordination.

Useful links

The original article on OECD Insights, including links and supplementary material, can be found here: *http://wp.me/p2v6oD-2AY*

The full series can be found here: *http://oecdinsights.org/?s=NAEC+complexity*

Economic complexity, institutions and income inequality

by César Hidalgo and Dominik Hartmann, Macro Connections,
The MIT Media Lab

Is a country's ability to generate and distribute income determined by its productive structure? Decades ago Simon Kuznets proposed an inverted-u-shaped relationship describing the connection between a country's average level of income and its level of income inequality. *Kuznets' curve* suggested that income inequality would first rise and then fall as countries' income moved from low to high. Yet, the curve has proven difficult to verify empirically. The inverted-u-shaped relationship fails to hold when several Latin American countries are removed from the sample, and in recent decades, the upward side of the Kuznets curve has vanished as inequality in many low-income countries has *increased*. Moreover, several East-Asian economies have grown from low to middle incomes while reducing income inequality.

Together, these findings undermine the empirical robustness of Kuznets' curve, and indicate that GDP per capita is a measure of economic development that is insufficient to explain variations in income inequality. This agrees with recent work arguing that inequality depends not only on a country's rate or stage of growth, but also on its type of growth and institutions. Hence, we should expect that more nuanced measures of economic development, such as those focused on the types of products a country exports, should provide information on the connection between economic development and inequality that transcends the limitations of aggregate output measures such as GDP.

Scholars have argued that income inequality depends on a variety of factors, from an economy's factor endowments, geography, and institutions, to its historical trajectories, changes in technology, and returns to capital. The combination of these factors should be expressed in the mix of products that a country makes. For example, colonial economies that specialised in a narrow set of agricultural or mineral products tend to have more unequal distributions of political power, human capital, and wealth. Conversely, sophisticated products, like medical imaging devices or electronic components, are typically produced in diversified economies that require more inclusive institutions. Complex industries and complex economies thrive when workers are able to contribute their creative input to the activities of firms.

This suggests a model of heterogeneous industries in which firms survive only when they are able to adopt or discover the institutions and human capital that work best in that industry. According to this model, the composition of products that a country exports should tell us about a country's institutions and about the quality of its human capital. This model would also suggest that a country's mix of products should provide information that explains inequality and that might escape aggregate measures of development such as GDP, average years of schooling, or survey-based measures of formal and informal institutions.

With our colleagues from the MIT Media Lab, we used the Economic Complexity Index (ECI) to capture information about an economy's level of development which is different from that captured in measures of income. Economic complexity is a measure of the knowledge in a society that gets translated into the products it makes. The most complex products are sophisticated chemicals and machinery, whereas the least complex products are raw materials or simple agricultural products. The economic complexity of a country depends on the complexity of the products it exports. A country is considered complex if it exports not only highly complex products but also a large number of different products. To calculate the economic complexity of a country, we measure the average ubiquity of the products it exports, then the average diversity of the countries that make those products, and so forth.

For example, in 2012, Chile's average income per capita and years of schooling (USD 21 044 at PPP in current 2012 USD and 9.8 mean years of schooling) were comparable to Malaysia's income per capita and schooling (USD 22 314 and 9.5), even though Malaysia ranked 24th in the ECI ranking while Chile ranked 72nd. The rankings reflect differences in these countries' export structure: Chile largely exports natural resources, while Malaysia exports a diverse range of electronics and machinery. Moreover, these differences in the ECI ranking also point more accurately to differences in these countries' level of income inequality. Chile's inequality as measured through the Gini coefficient (0.49) is significantly higher than that of Malaysia (0.39).

We separated the correlation between economic complexity and income inequality from the correlation between income inequality and average income, population, human capital (measured by average years of schooling), export concentration, and formal institutions. Our results document a strong and robust correlation between the economic complexity index and income inequality. This relationship is robust even after controlling for measures of income, education, and institutions, and the relationship has remained strong over the last fifty years. Results also show that increases in economic complexity tend to be accompanied by decreases in income inequality.

Our findings do not mean that productive structures solely determine a country's level of income inequality. On the contrary, a more likely explanation is that productive structures represent a high-resolution expression of a number of factors, from institutions to education, that co-evolve with the mix of products that a country exports and with the inclusiveness of its economy. Still, because of this co-evolution, our findings emphasize that productive structures are not only associated with income and economic growth, but also with how income is distributed.

We advance methods that enable a more fine-grained perspective on the relationship between productive structures and income inequality. The method is based on introducing the Product Gini Index, or PGI, which estimates the expected level of inequality for the countries exporting a given product. Overlaying PGI values on the network of related products allows us to create maps that can be used to anticipate how changes in a country's productive structure will affect its level of income inequality. These maps provide means for researchers and policy makers to explore and compare the complex co-evolution of productive structures, institutions and income inequality for hundreds of economies.

Useful links

The original article on OECD Insights, including links and supplementary material, can be found here: *http://wp.me/p2v6oD-2CN*

The full series can be found here: *http://oecdinsights.org/?s=NAEC+complexity*

Crowds, consensus and complexity in economic forecasting

by Brian Dowd, FocusEconomics

Predicting the future behaviour of anything, much less something as complex and enormous as an entire economy, is not an easy task. Accurate forecasts, therefore, are often in short supply. Economies are complex systems in perpetual motion, and extrapolating behaviours and relationships from past economic cycles into the next one is tremendously complicated. Moreover, and perhaps surprisingly, forecasting is difficult due to the vast amount of raw economic data available. In an ideal world, economic forecasts would consider all of the information available. In the real world, however, that is nearly impossible, as information is scattered in myriad news articles, government communications, and so on, as well as the mountain of raw data.

Although some might consider having all of that information an advantage, nothing could be further from the truth. The thousands of indicators and data available tend to produce a vast amount of statistical noise, making the establishment of meaningful relations of causation between variables a serious challenge. And, of course, we cannot forget the inherent uncertainty in forecasting, something that forecasters must take into account and which creates even more noise to deal with.

The question then becomes, is there a way to cancel out all of that noise to get a more accurate forecast? This is where "the wisdom of the crowds" comes in. Sir Francis Galton, a Victorian polymath, was the first to note the wisdom of the crowds at a livestock fair he visited in 1906. Fairgoers were given the opportunity to guess the weight of an ox, with the best guess winning a prize. Galton hypothesised that not one person would get the answer right, but that everyone would get it right. It's not as contradictory as it sounds. Over 750 participants made their guesses and unsurprisingly no one guessed the weight perfectly. However, when Galton calculated the mean average of all of the guesses, incredibly, it turned out to be the exact weight of the ox: 1 198 pounds.

The basic idea of the wisdom of the crowds is that the average of the answers of a group of individuals is often more accurate than the answer of any one individual, as in Galton's experiment. The wisdom of the crowds' accuracy increases with the number of participants and the diversity of the expertise of each individual participant.

So what does the wisdom of the crowds have to do with economic forecasting? Remember all of that noise that makes economic forecasting so difficult and affects accuracy? The theory is that idiosyncratic noise is associated with any one individual answer and by taking the average of multiple answers the noise tends to cancel itself out, presenting a far more accurate picture.

Sometimes also referred to as simply combining forecasts, the consensus forecast borrows from the same idea of Galton's wisdom of the crowds. It is essentially the average of forecasts from various sources. A great deal of empirical research over the last few decades shows that averaging multiple forecasts cancels out the statistical noise to yield a more accurate forecast. That said, it is possible for an individual forecast to beat the consensus, but, it is unlikely that the same forecaster will consistently do so one forecast period after another. Moreover, those individual forecasts that do happen to beat the consensus in one period are impossible to pick out ahead of time since they vary significantly from period to period.

A practical example shows the advantages of the consensus forecast. The Consensus Forecast for Malaysia's 2015 GDP taken in January 2015 was 5.1%. In March 2016, the actual reading came out at 5.0%. As expected, a few forecasts were closer to the end result than the Consensus, but as already mentioned, it would be impossible to know which forecasts those will be until after the fact. Another way to look at it is to compare different individual forecasts with what actually happened, as we did for 25 economic analysts' forecasts for Malaysia's 2015 GDP in January of 2015. By March 2016, the maximum forecast from this group turned out to be 16% above the actual reading with the minimum 10% below it. The consensus was only 1.9% above the actual reading. By taking the average of all forecasts, the upside and downside errors of the different forecasts mostly cancelled each other out. As a result, the consensus forecast was much closer to the actual reading than the majority of the individual forecasts.

Whether they are consensus forecasts or individual forecasts or any other kind of forecast, predicting the future is seldom going to be perfect. In the Malaysia example, the Consensus wasn't spot on, but it did certainly reduce the margin of error. There is almost always going to be some error, but reducing that error is the key, and more often than not, it will result in a more accurate forecast. The consensus not only reduces the margin of error, it also provides some consistency and reliability. The forecasts from individual analysts can vary significantly from one to another, whereas the consensus will consistently provide accurate forecasts.

Forecasting is a science, but it isn't an exact science. They may not be perfect, but forecasts are still very important to businesses and governments, as they shed light on the future, helping them to make vital decisions on strategy, plans and budgets. So, should you trust forecasts? True, forecasting is complicated and, yes, forecasts are notoriously inaccurate and there are few ways to consistently improve forecast accuracy. The point is, however, that forecasts don't necessarily need to be perfect to be useful. They just need to be as accurate as possible. One such way to do so is leveraging the wisdom of a crowd of analysts to produce a consensus forecast.

As French mathematician, physicist and philosopher Henri Poincaré put it, "It is far better to foresee even without certainty than not to foresee at all." The consensus forecast is a more accurate way to "foresee."

Useful links

The original article on OECD Insights, including links and supplementary material, can be found here: *http://wp.me/p2v6oD-2Mn*

The full series can be found here: *http://oecdinsights.org/?s=NAEC+complexity*

Complexity and the financial system

A complex global financial system

by Adrian Blundell-Wignall, Special Advisor
to the OECD Secretary-General on Financial and Enterprise Affairs

Global finance is the perfect example of a complex system, consisting as it does of a highly interconnected system of sub-systems featuring tipping points, emergence, asymmetries, unintended consequences, a "parts-within-parts" structure (to quote Herbert Simon), and all the other defining characteristics of complexity. It is shaped by numerous internal and external trends and shocks that it also influences and generates in turn. And as the system (in most parts) also reacts to predictions about it, it can be called a "level two" chaotic system (as described, e.g. by Yuval Harari)

Numerous developments combined to contribute to the 2008 crisis and several of them led to structures and institutions that might pose problems again. Two important trends that would play a huge role in the crisis were the opening up of OECD economies to international trade and investment after 1945, and rapid advances in digital technology and networks. These trends brought a greater complexity of financial products and structures needed to navigate this new world, going well beyond the needs to meet the increased demand for cross-border banking to include new products that would facilitate hedging of exchange rate and credit default risks; financial engineering to match maturities required by savers and investors, and to take advantage of different tax and regulatory regimes; mergers and acquisitions not only of businesses, but of stock exchanges and related markets with global capabilities; and new platforms and technological developments to handle the trading of volatile new products.

The freeing up of financial markets followed the opening of goods markets, and in some respects was the necessary counterpart of it. However, the process went very far, and by the end of the 1990s policies encouraged the "financial supermarket" model, and by 2004 bank capital rules became materially more favourable to bank leverage as did rule changes for investment banks. The banking system became the epicentre of the global financial crisis, because of the under-pricing of risk, essentially due to poor micro-prudential regulation, excessive leverage, and too-big-to-fail business models. The rise of the institutional investor, the expansion of leverage and derivatives, the general deepening of financial markets and technological advances led to innovations not only in products but also in how securities are traded, for example high-frequency trading. The increasing separation of owners from the governance of companies also added a new layer of complexity compounding some of these issues (passive funds, exchange-traded funds, or ETFs, lending agent's custody, re-hypothecation, advisors and consultants are all in the mix).

The trends towards openness in OECD economies were not mirrored in emerging market economies (EMEs) generally, and in Asia in particular. Capital controls remained strong in some EMEs despite a strengthening and better regulated domestic financial system. Furthermore, capital control measures have often supported a managed exchange rate regime in relation to the US dollar. When countries intervene to fix their currencies versus the dollar, they acquire US dollars and typically recycle these into holdings of US Treasuries, very liquid and low-risk securities. There are two important effects of the increasingly large size of "dollar bloc" EME's: first, they compress Treasury yields as the stock of their holdings grows, second, their foreign exchange intervention means that the US economy faces a misalignment of its exchange rates vis-à-vis these trading partners.

Low interest rates, together with the more compressed yields on Treasury securities, have encouraged investors to search for higher-risk and higher-yield products. In "risk-on" periods this contributes to increased inflows into EME high-yield credit which, in turn, contributes to more foreign exchange intervention and increased capital control measures. The potential danger is that in "risk-off" periods, the attempt to sell these illiquid assets will result in huge pressures on EME funding and a great deal of volatility in financial markets.

The euro affects financial stability too, often in unexpected ways… European countries trade not only with each other but with the rest of the world. However, the north of Europe is, through global value chains, more vertically integrated into strongly growing Asia due to the demands for high-quality technology, infrastructure, and other investment goods, while the south of Europe is competing with EMEs to a greater degree in lower-level manufacturing trade. Asymmetric real shocks to different euro area regions, such as divergent fiscal policy or changes in EME competitiveness, mean that a one-size-fits-all approach to monetary policy creates economic divergence. Resulting bad loans feed back into financial fragility issues, and interconnectedness adds to the complexity of the problem.

Population ageing adds to these concerns, notably due to the interactions among longer life spans, low yields on the government bonds that underpin pension funds, and lack of saving by the less wealthy who were hardest hit by the crisis and may also suffer from future changes in employment and career structures. To meet yield targets, institutions have taken on more risk in products that are often less transparent and where providers are trying to create "artificial liquidity" that does not exist in the underlying securities and assets.

However big and complex the financial system, though, it is not an end in itself. Its role should be to help fund the economic growth and jobs that will contribute to well-being. But despite all the interconnectedness, paradoxically, as the *OECD Business and Finance Outlook 2016* argues, fragmentation is blocking business investment and productivity growth.

In financial markets, information technology and regulatory reforms have paved the way for fragmentation with respect to an increased number of stock trading venues and created so-called "dark trading" pools. Differences in regulatory requirements and disclosure among trading venues raise concerns about stock market transparency and equal treatment of investors. Also, corporations may be affected negatively if speed and complexity is rewarded over long-term investing.

Different legal regimes across countries and in the growing network of international investment treaties also fragment the business environment. National laws in different countries sanction foreign bribery with uneven and often insufficient severity, and many investment treaties have created rules that can fragment companies with respect to their investors and disrupt established rules on corporate governance and corporate finance.

Complexity is in the nature of the financial system, but if we want this system to play its role in funding inclusive, sustainable growth, we need to put these fragmented pieces back together in a more harmonious way.

Useful links

The original article on OECD Insights, including links and supplementary material, can be found here: *http://wp.me/p2v6oD-2JC*

The full series can be found here: *http://oecdinsights.org/?s=NAEC+complexity*

Complexity and better financial regulation

by Harald Stieber, Economic Analysis and Evaluation Unit,
DG FISMA, European Commission

The financial crisis of 2007/08 was not caused by complexity alone. It was caused by rapidly increasing financial leverage until a breaking point was reached. While the mostly short-term debt used for leveraging up consists of "run-prone contracts", the precise location of that breaking point had to be discovered in real time and space rather than in a controlled simulation environment. Also, the complex dynamic patterns that emerged as the crisis unfolded showed that little had been known about how an increasingly complex financial system would transmit stress. The sequence of markets being impacted and the speed of risk propagation across different markets and market infrastructures was not known beforehand and had to be discovered "on the fly". Our ignorance with respect to these static and dynamic properties of the system reflects deep-rooted issues linked to data governance, modelling capabilities, and policy design (in that order).

From a policy perspective, the crisis revealed that several parts of the financial ecosystem remained outside the regulatory perimeter. As a result, the public good of financial stability was not provided any longer to a sufficient degree in all circumstances. However, the regulatory agenda that followed, under a principles-based approach co-ordinated at the level of the newly created G20, while closing many important regulatory gaps, also created increasing regulatory complexity.

Regulatory complexity can also increase risks to financial stability. Higher compliance cost can induce avoidance behaviour, which makes financial regulation less effective as regulated entities and agents will engage in regulatory arbitrage as well as in seeking to escape the regulatory perimeter altogether via financial innovation. Until recently, at least the largest financial institutions were considered to "like" regulatory complexity.

However, the perception of complexity in the financial industry is changing. Complexity cannot be gamed any longer as compliance cost and risk of fines have increased. One of the clearest statements in that direction came in the form of a letter from financial trading associations that we at the European Commission received (together with all main regulators) on 11 June 2015. In their letter, the associations called for co-ordinated action in the area of financial (data) standards that would reduce complexity to a level that could again be managed by the sector.

The European Commission's Better Regulation agenda has at its heart the principle that existing rules need to be evaluated in a continuous manner to assess their effectiveness[1] as well as their efficiency[2]. Under this agenda, the Commission launched a public consultation in 2015 calling on stakeholders to provide evidence on 15 issues with a strong focus on the cumulative impact of financial regulation in place. The purpose was to identify possible overlaps, inconsistencies, duplications, or gaps in the financial regulatory framework which had increased considerably in complexity. The area of (data) reporting emerged as a major area where responses pointed to important possible future gains in regulatory effectiveness and efficiency.

Regulatory reporting has seen massive changes as the lack of relevant data at the level of supervisory authorities had been identified as a major source of risk during the crisis. Especially, legislation in the area of financial markets such as the European Market Infrastructure Regulation (EMIR), but also *MiFID/R*, employed a different approach to regulatory reporting compared to existing reporting obligations for regulated financial institutions (e.g. COREP, FINREP). EMIR puts the focus on the individual financial transaction (of financial derivatives traded over-the-counter rather than on a regulated exchange), with reporting at the most granular level of the individual financial contract. Reporting under EMIR started to be

1. Effectiveness: Does the impact observed on the ground correspond to the outcome aimed for by the EU co-legislators?
2. Efficiency: Is the desired regulatory outcome achieved at lowest possible compliance cost?

rolled out in several phases from February 2014 and is still ongoing, starting from the most standardised contracts and continuing to the least standardised ones. This approach is extended to a broader class of instruments under MiFID/R.

This granular approach to regulatory reporting holds tremendous promise from a complexity science perspective. It could, at some point, allow the mapping of the financial ecosystem from bottom-up, as well as further the development of a Global Systems Science policy-making process. However, to arrive at more evidence-based, data-driven policies, data governance, and more precisely financial data standards, will have to be adapted to the increasingly granular data-reporting environment.

Data governance requires robust financial data standards that keep up with technological change. We see a few precise implications at this stage what standards need to do in that respect. Financial contract data is Big Data. Financial data standards produce small data from Big Data. They add structure and scalability in both directions.

In a follow-up project to the call for evidence, we are therefore looking at different ways how financial data standards and regulatory technology can help achieve Better Regulation objectives. These possible ways comprise the definition of core data methodologies, the development of data point models, exploring the use of algorithmic standards, as well as possible uses of distributed ledger and decentralised consensus technologies. We cannot say at this stage if the vision of a "run-free financial system" is within our reach in the medium-term. But the resilience properties of the internet are one possible guide how technology could help regulatory reporting achieve its objectives in a much more powerful way in the future that will at the same time acknowledge the complexity of our subject matter.

Useful links

The original article on OECD Insights, including links and supplementary material, can be found here: *http://wp.me/p2v6oD-2B7*

The full series can be found here: *http://oecdinsights.org/?s=NAEC+complexity*

Agent-based models to help economics do a better job

by Richard Bookstaber, University of California

Economics has not done a very good job of dealing with crises. I think this is because there are four characteristics of human experience that manifest themselves in crises and that cannot be addressed well by the methods of traditional economics.

The first of these is computational irreducibility. You may be able to reduce the behaviour of a simple system to a mathematical description that provides a shortcut to predicting its future behaviour; the way a map shows that following a road gets you to a town without having to physically travel the road first. Unfortunately, for many systems, as Stephen Wolfram argues, you only know what is going to happen by faithfully reproducing the path the system takes to its end point, through simulation and observation, with no chance of getting to the final state before the system itself. It's a bit like the map Borges describes in On Rigor in Science, where "the Map of the Empire had the size of the Empire itself and coincided with it point by point". Not being able to reduce the economy to a computation means you can't predict it using analytical methods, but economics requires that you can.

The second characteristic property is emergence. Emergent phenomena occur when the overall effect of individuals' actions is qualitatively different from what each of the individuals are doing. You cannot anticipate the outcome for the whole system on the basis of the actions of its individual members because the large system will show properties its individual members do not have. For example, some people pushing others in a crowd may lead to nothing or it may lead to a stampede with people getting crushed, despite nobody wanting this or acting intentionally to produce it. Likewise no one decides to precipitate a financial crisis, and indeed at the level of the individual firms, decisions generally are made to take prudent action to avoid the costly effects of a crisis. But what is locally stable can become globally unstable.

The name for the third characteristic, non-ergodicity, comes from the German physicist Ludwig Boltzmann who defined as "ergodic" a concept in statistical mechanics whereby a single trajectory, continued long enough at constant energy, would be representative of an isolated system as a whole, from the Greek *ergon* energy, and *odos* path. The mechanical processes that drive of our physical world are ergodic, as are many biological processes. We can predict how a ball will move when struck without knowing how it got into its present position – past doesn't matter. But the past matters in social processes and you cannot simply extrapolate it to know the future. The dynamics of a financial crisis are not reflected in the pre-crisis period for instance because financial markets are constantly innovating, so the future may look nothing like the past.

Radical uncertainty completes our quartet. It describes surprises – outcomes or events that are unanticipated, that cannot be put into a probability distribution because they are outside our list of things that might occur. Electric power, the atomic bomb, or the internet are examples from the past, and of course by definition we don't know what the future will be. As Keynes put it, "There is no scientific basis to form any calculable probability whatever. We simply do not know." Economists also talk about "Knightian uncertainty", after Frank Knight, who distinguished between risk, for example gambling in a casino where we don't know the outcome but can calculate the odds; and what he called "true uncertainty" where we can't know everything that would be needed to calculate the odds. This in fact is the human condition. We don't know where we are going, and we don't know who we will be when we get there. The reality of humanity means that a mechanistic approach to economics will fail.

So is there any hope of understanding what's happening in our irreducible, emergent, non-ergodic, radically uncertain economy? Yes, if we use methods that are more robust, that are not embedded in the standard rational expectations, optimisation mode of economics. To deal with crises, we need methods that deal with computational irreducibility; recognise emergence; allow for the fact that not even the present is reflected in the past, never mind the future; and that can deal with radical uncertainty. Agent-based modelling could be a step in the right direction.

Agent-based models (ABM) use a dynamic system of interacting, autonomous agents to allow macroscopic behaviour to emerge from microscopic rules. The models specify rules that dictate how agents will act based on various inputs. Each agent individually assesses its situation and makes decisions on the basis of its rules. Starlings swirling in the sky (a "murmuration") is a good illustration. The birds appear to operate as a system, yet the flight is based on the decisions of the individual birds. Building a macro, top-down model will miss the reality of the situation, because at the macro level the movements of the flock are complex, non-linear, yet are not based on any system-wide programme. But you can model the murmuration based on simple rules as to how a bird reacts to the distance, speed and direction of the other birds, and heads for the perceived centre of the flock in its immediate neighbourhood.

Likewise, the agent-based approach recognises that individuals interact and in interacting change the environment, leading to the next course of interaction. It operates without the fiction of a representative consumer or investor who is as unerringly right as a mathematical model can dream. It allows for construction of a narrative – unique to the particular circumstances in the real world – in which the system may jump the tracks and career down the mountainside. This narrative gives us a shot at pulling the system back safely.

In short, agent-based economics arrives ready to face the real world, the world that is amplified and distorted during times of crisis. This is a new paradigm rooted in pragmatism and in the complexities of being human.

Useful links

The original article on OECD Insights, including links and supplementary material, can be found here: *http://wp.me/p2v6oD-2MX*

The full series can be found here: *http://oecdinsights.org/?s=NAEC+complexity*

Applications of complexity theory

Urbanisation and complex Systems

by Colin Harrison, IBM Distinguished Engineer Emeritus (retired),
formerly lead the development of technical strategy
for IBM's Smarter Cities initiative

The city is humanity's greatest invention. An artificial ecosystem that enables millions of people to live in close proximity and to collaborate in the creation of new forms of value. While cities were invented many millennia ago, their economic importance has increased dramatically since the Industrial Revolution until they now account for the major fraction of the global economy. All human life is there and so the study of cities crosses boundaries among economics, finance, engineering, ecology, sociology, anthropology, and, well, almost all forms of knowledge. Yet, while we have great knowledge in each of these domains individually, we have little scientific knowledge of how they come together in the overall system of systems that is a city. In brief: How does a city work?

Such knowledge would be helpful in the coming decades. In the last sixty to seventy years, globalisation has spread the Industrial Revolution ever more widely, creating in cities new opportunities that attract hundreds of millions of internal and international migrants. This process is lifting many of these migrants out of deep poverty, while causing cities from London to Nairobi to struggle in differing ways with the unending influx.

Further, cities are responsible for large fractions of greenhouse gas emissions, for the consumption of natural resources such as water and air, and the resulting discharges of pollution into the environment. If the battle against climate change is to be won, it will be won in cities. Cities are also the principal centres for innovation and economic development, both of which are needed to continue lifting migrants out of poverty.

While the roots of urban planning can be traced back more than three thousand years in terms of the master plans of cities, it was the tremendous growth of cities in the late 19th century that transformed that field into considering the many services and affordances that are required for urban dwellers. But urban planning emerged mainly from the humanities and works primarily through extensive case studies, although it has adopted many digital tools. The notion of the city as an object of scientific study is more recent and still in its infancy, triggered in part by developments in complexity theory such as network theory, scaling laws, and systems science, and the growing availability of urban data.

Urban scaling laws have been explored at least since the early 20th century, when cities were found seen to be an example of Zipf's law. In this case Zipf's Law states that "for most countries, the number of cities with population greater than S is proportional to 1/S". The understanding of scaling was greatly expanded in recent years by the works of West and Bettencourt and Batty. Their work showed that many properties of cities such as the number or lengths of roadways, the numbers of amenities such as restaurants, and so forth follow scaling laws over population ranges from ten thousand to tens of millions. Moreover these scaling laws have exponents in the ranges 0.85 to 1.15 that show large cities to be more productive, innovative, efficient in energy consumption, expensive, but also better paying than small cities. Likewise negative attributes such as crime, disease, and pollution also scale superlinearly, that is they don't rise in strict proportion to the increase in city size. For example, GDP is proportional to the Size (S) of a city raised to a power that is slightly greater than 1, thus $S^{1.15}$, while other attributes like energy consumption per capita scale sublinearly, at $S^{0.85}$. Network laws also describe well the evolution over long time scales of roadways and railways in cities.

While scaling laws and network laws have great descriptive power, opinions vary on whether they apply across different countries or have predictive power. That is, the scaling of attributes is a snapshot of frequency versus size at a given time. If a city grows and "moves up the scale", it may not achieve, in the short term, all of the positive benefits and negative impacts described. Nor do the laws provide explanations for the observed behaviours. Nonetheless, this is an important area for planners and developers seeing their cities growing or shrinking.

As urban data has become more pervasive, it is now possible to study cities as complex systems of interactions. We may view the city as a myriad of interactions among its inhabitants, its infrastructures and affordances, its natural environment, and its public, private, and civic organisations. Some of these interactions involve the exchange of goods or services for money, but many of them involve the exchange or transmission of information, enabling inhabitants and organisations to make choices. Public transportation is often studied in this way, revealing for example that small- and medium-sized cities evolve networks enabling commuting between small numbers of residential and business districts, while very large cities, such as London, have much richer networks that permit greater flexibility in where people live and work.

The operation of cities is also modelled using synthetic populations of software agents that represent the distribution of behaviours or preferences of much larger, real populations. Such agent-based models, with agents representing patterns of origin, destination, travel times, and modality preferences, are used to examine the overall impact of new services such as London's Crossrail.

As the Internet of Things provides greater visibility into how inhabitants choose to exploit the opportunities offered by a given city, we may hope to discover abstract principles about how cities work. We may envision being able to construct agent-based models representing the complete spectrum of choices a city's inhabitants make at timescales from minutes to years and spatial scales from meters to kilometres. Equally, given the increasing availability of real-time information, we might hope one day to understand the effective use of a city's services in terms of a Nash Equilibrium, a game theory concept (often used to describe poker games), where no player can gain anything by changing their chosen strategy if other players don't change theirs – all the players' strategies are optimal. These are far in the future, but the European Commission's Global Systems Science programme is the beginning of that journey.

Useful links

The original article on OECD Insights, including links and supplementary material, can be found here: *http://wp.me/p2v6oD-2Cx*

The full series can be found here: *http://oecdinsights.org/?s=NAEC+complexity*

Big Data, complexity theory and urban development

by Ricardo Herranz, Managing Director, Nommon Solutions and Technologies, Madrid

We are living in the era of cities: more than 50% of the world population is already living in urban areas, and most forecasts indicate that, by the end of this century, the world's population will be almost entirely urban. In this context, there is an emerging view that the global challenges of poverty eradication, environmental sustainability, climate change, and sustainable and secure energy are all intimately linked to cities, which are simultaneously places where these global problems emerge and solutions can be found. In the short term, cities are facing the major challenge of overcoming the financial and economic crisis and emerging stronger from it. In the long term, they need to deal with structural challenges related to globalisation, climate change, pressure on resources, demographic change, migration, and social segregation and polarisation. Many of these challenges are shared by cities from developed and developing countries, while others depend on geographical, institutional, socio-economic and cultural differences.

When addressing these problems, policy makers and society at large face a number of fundamental problems. The many components of the urban system are strongly interwoven, giving rise to complex dynamics and making it difficult to anticipate the impact and unintended consequences of public action. Cities are not closed systems, but they are part of systems of cities. Urban development policies are subject to highly distributed, multi-level decision processes and have a profound impact on a wide variety of stakeholders, often with conflicting or contradictory objectives.

In the past few years we have seen the emergence of concepts such as the smart city, urban informatics, urban analytics and citizen science, which are seen to hold great promise for improving the functioning of cities. However, arguably most of this potential still remains to be realised. The concept of the smart city has been coined as a fusion of ideas about how information and communication technologies can help address critical issues relating to cities.

Essential to this concept is the notion of an integrated approach to the synergies and trade-offs between different policy domains that are closely interrelated, but have traditionally been addressed separately, such as land use, transport and energy. This integrated approach would be facilitated by the ability to analyse the increasingly large data streams generated by the ubiquitous sensorisation of the built environment and the pervasive use of personal mobile devices. In parallel, smart devices and social media are also producing new forms of public participation in urban planning. The opportunities are vast, but so are the challenges.

Much hope has been placed in the explosion of Big Data for establishing the foundations of a new science of cities. During the last 20 years, the dominant trend in urban modelling has changed from aggregate, equilibrium models to bottom-up dynamic models (activity-based and agent-based models) that seek to represent cities in more disaggregated and heterogeneous terms. This increasing model sophistication comes with the need for abundant, fine-grained data for model calibration and validation, hindering the operational use of state-of-the-art modelling approaches. The emergence of new sources of Big Data is enabling the collection of spatio-temporal data about urban activity with an unprecedented level of detail, providing us with information that was not available from surveys or census data. This has already yielded important practical advances in fields like transportation planning, but it is more questionable, at least for the moment, that Big Data has produced substantial advances in our understanding of cities. In principle, the potential is there: while research on cities has historically relied on cross-sectional demographic and economic datasets, often consisting of relatively small samples, we have now large-scale, detailed longitudinal data that can allow us to test new hypotheses about urban structure and dynamics. On the other hand, there is a risk that Big Data leads to a shift in focus towards short-term, predictive, non-explanatory models, abandoning theory. Connecting the smart city and Big Data movements with the knowledge developed in the last decades in fields like regional science, urban economics and transportation modelling appears as an essential condition to overcome this problem and take advantage of the opportunities offered by Big Data for the formulation of better theories and policy approaches.

Both empirical work and theoretical advances are needed to cope with the new challenges raised by energy scarcity and climate change, emerging technologies like self-driving cars, and the changes in social relationships, the new activities and the new forms of sharing economy enabled by social media and electronic communications, among other factors that are leading to profound changes in urban structure and dynamics. Equally challenging is to integrate data and models into governance processes: policy assessment and participatory planning are still largely based on qualitative considerations, and there is a sense that state-of-the-art urban models are immature with respect to institutional integration and operational use. New forms of data sharing and visualisation, digital participation and citizens' engagement are promising tools to tackle this question, but here again, we still have to figure out how to share data and specialised knowledge in a form that fluidly intersects participatory decision making process and bridges the gap between implicit and explicit knowledge. Recent advances in areas such as network theory, agent-based computational modelling and group decision theory, and more generally the intrinsically holistic and eclectic approach advocated by complexity science, appear as a suitable framework for the development of a new science of cities which can in turn lead to new advances in the way cities are planned and managed, allowing us to address the enormous challenges related to urban development in the 21st century.

Useful links

The original article on OECD Insights, including links and supplementary material, can be found here: *http://wp.me/p2v6oD-2Di*

The full series can be found here: *http://oecdinsights.org/?s=NAEC+complexity*

Innovation and complexity

by Andrew Wyckoff, Director, OECD Directorate for Science, Technology and Innovation

Since its creation in 1961, the OECD has influenced how governments approach science, technology and innovation, and how economics as a discipline tries to understand these phenomena. The OECD Working Party of National Experts on Science and Technology Indicators (NESTI) was created in 1962, and in 1963, *Science, economic growth and government policy* convinced governments that science policy should be linked to economic policy. In 1971 *Science, growth and society* (also called the *Brook Report* after the Chair, Harvey Brooks) anticipated many of today's concerns by emphasising the need to involve citizens in assessing the consequences of developing and using new technologies.

For many experts though, the major contribution was the concept of national innovation systems, presented in 1992 in a landmark publication, *Technology and the Economy: The Key Relationships*. The origins of the concept go back to the 1970s crisis, which had provoked an in-depth re-examination of previous economic thinking on how growth came about and why growth in productivity was slowing. A 1980 OECD report, *Technical Change and Economic Policy*, is now widely recognised as the first major policy document to challenge the macroeconomic interpretations of the 1970s crisis, and to emphasise the role of technological factors in finding solutions, arguing for instance that innovation can be more powerful than wage competitiveness in stimulating an economy.

Economists working at the OECD were pioneers of a new approach that saw innovation not as something linear but as an ecosystem involving interactions among existing knowledge, research, and invention; potential markets; and the production process. In national innovation strategies, one of the key issues is the interactions among the different actors: companies, public research institutions, intermediary organisations, and so on. And contrary to the dominant thinking in policy circles in the 1980s and early 1990s, the OECD also saw it as something that governments should play a central role in – hence the term national innovation strategy.

Today, services are becoming the focus of innovation, with some companies even blurring the distinction between the value-added of products and services, smartphones being a good example. This is a logical outcome of the increasing digitalisation of the economy. Digital technologies are now so ubiquitous that it is easy to forget how recent they are. The World Wide Web we know today for example was created in the 1990s, and Microsoft thought it was possible to launch a rival to Internet (called MSN) as late as 1995. Google was only founded in 1998 and it would be 6 years before it went public.

With the digital economy and society coming so far in such a short time, it is hard to predict what they will look like in the future. We can however identify some of the drivers of change. Big Data will be among the most important. In *The phenomenon of data-driven innovation*, the OECD quotes figures suggesting that more than 2.5 exabytes (EB, a billion gigabytes) of data are generated every single day, the equivalent of 167 000 times the information contained in all the books in the US Library of Congress. The world's largest retail company, Walmart, already handles more than 1 million customer transactions every hour. Because so many new data are available, it will be possible to develop new models exploiting the power of a complexity approach to improve understanding in the social sciences, including economics. Also, the policy-making process may benefit from new ways of collecting data on policies themselves and vastly improving our evaluation capabilities.

The analysis of data (often in real time), increasingly from smart devices embedded in the Internet of Things opens new opportunities for value creation through optimisation of production processes and the creation of new services. This "industrial Internet" is creating its own complex systems, empowering autonomous machines and networks that can learn and make decisions independently of human involvement. This can generate new products and markets, but it can also create chaos in existing markets, as various financial flash crashes have shown.

Two sets of challenges, or tensions, need to be addressed by policy makers to maximise the benefits of digitally-driven innovation, and mitigate the associated economic and societal risks. The first is to promote "openness" in the global data ecosystem and thus the free flow of data across nations, sectors, and organisations while at the same time addressing individuals' and organisations' opposing interests (in particular protecting their privacy and their intellectual property). The second set of tensions requires finding policies to activate the enablers of digital-driven innovation, and at the same time addressing the effects of the "creative destruction" induced by this innovation. Moreover, there is a question concerning the efficacy of national policies as digital-driven innovation is global by definition. As a policy maker you can promote something in your country, but the spillovers in terms of employment or markets can be somewhere else.

With so many new technologies being introduced, more firms and countries being integrated into global value chains, and workers becoming more highly educated everywhere, you would expect productivity growth to be surging. In fact it is slowing. But that average trend hides the true picture according to an OECD study on The Future of Productivity. Labour productivity in the globally most productive firms ("global frontier" firms) grew at an average annual rate of 3.5% in the manufacturing sector over the 2000s, compared to 0.5% for non-frontier firms.

Diffusion of the know-how from the pioneering frontier firms to the bulk of the economy hasn't occurred – either because channels are blocked or because we are in a transformative period and the expertise for how best to exploit the technologies is still in the heads of a few. Most likely, it is a combination of the two. We therefore have to help the global frontier firms to continue innovating and facilitate the diffusion of new technologies and innovations from the global frontier firms to firms at the national frontier. We can try to create a market environment where the most productive firms are allowed to thrive, thereby facilitating the more widespread penetration of available technologies and innovations. And we have to improve the matching of skills to jobs to better use the pool of available talent in the economy, and allow skilled people to change jobs, spreading the know-how as they move.

In a complex system, you can't forecast outcomes with any great degree of certainty, but many of the unintended outcomes of interactions in the innovation system are beneficial. The policies mentioned above would each be useful in themselves and would hopefully reinforce each other beneficially.

Useful links

The original article on OECD Insights, including links and supplementary material, can be found here: *http://wp.me/p2v6oD-2Ff*

The full series can be found here: *http://oecdinsights.org/?s=NAEC+complexity*

Governing education in a complex world

by Tracey Burns, Project Leader, *OECD Directorate for Education and Skills*

The famous slogan "KISS" urges listeners to "Keep it simple, stupid!" However, modern policy making is increasingly discovering that *not* keeping it simple – in fact, embracing the *complex* – is essential to understanding contemporary systems and making reform work.

Modern societies are made up of a growing number of diverse stakeholders who collaborate through formal and informal channels. The rapid advancement and reach of information and communication technologies has enabled them to play a much more immediate role in decision-making while at the same time the delivery of public services has become more decentralised.

This complexity brings a series of dynamics that the traditional policy cycle is not able to capture. This is not startling news: numerous critics have described the inadequacy of the traditional policy cycle in agriculture, medicine, and education for the last 30 years. What has changed, however, is a growing understanding across a much broader set of actors that we can no longer continue to operate using traditional linear models of reform.

This is not just a theoretical discussion: ignoring the dynamic nature of the governance process makes reform less effective. In education for instance, even very similar schools can react quite differently to the same intervention. A case study of the Netherlands demonstrated how some weak schools benefitted from being labelled as in need of improvement, coming together as a school community to set off a virtuous cycle to improve performance. In contrast other schools struggled when faced with the same label, with some descending into vicious cycles where teachers felt unmotivated, parents moved their children to another school, and overall performance declined. A simple model of reform and governance cannot account for this complexity.

How can complexity be identified? A seminal 2002 paper by Glouberman and Zimmerman distinguishes between three types of problems: the *simple*, the complicated, and the complex. A simple problem is, for example, baking a cake. For a first time baker, this is not easy, but with a recipe and the ingredients you can be relatively sure that you will succeed. Expertise here is helpful, but not required.

In contrast, a *complicated* problem would be sending a rocket to the moon. Here, formulas are essential and high level expertise is not only helpful, but necessary. However, rockets are similar to each other in critical ways, and once you have solved the original complicated problem, you can be reasonably certain that you'll be able to do it again.

Both simple and complicated problems can be contrasted with a *complex* problem, such as raising a child. As every parent knows, there is no recipe or formula that will ensure success. Bringing up one child provides useful experience, but it is no guarantee of success with another. This is because each child is unique and sometimes unpredictable. Solutions that may work in one case may only partially work, or not work at all, in another.

Returning to the failing school example, it was the unpredictability of the dynamics inherent in the response of the schools and their communities that rendered the problem complex as opposed to merely complicated. Acknowledging the complexity inherent in modern governance is thus an essential first step to effective reform.

Successful modern governance:

➤ *Focuses on processes, not structures.* Almost all governance structures can be successful under the right conditions. The number of levels, and the power at each level, is not what makes or breaks a good system. Rather, it is the strength of the alignment across the system, the involvement of actors, and the processes underlying governance and reform.

➤ *Is flexible and able to adapt to change and unexpected events.* Strengthening a system's ability to learn from feedback is a fundamental part of this process, and is also a necessary step to quality assurance and accountability.

➤ *Works through building capacity, stakeholder involvement and open dialogue.* However it is not rudderless: involvement of a broader range of stakeholders only works when there is a strategic vision and set of processes to harness their ideas and input.

➤ *Requires a whole of system approach.* This requires aligning policies, roles and responsibilities to improve efficiency and reduce potential overlap or conflict (e.g. between accountability and trust, or innovation and risk-avoidance).

➤ *Harnesses evidence and research to inform policy and reform.* A strong knowledge system combines descriptive system data, research findings and practitioner knowledge. The key knows what to use, why and how.

Creating the open, dynamic and strategic governance systems necessary for governing complex systems is not easy. Modern governance must be able to juggle the dynamism and complexity at the same time as it steers a clear course towards established goals. And with limited financial resources it must do this as efficiently as possible. Although a challenging task, it is a necessary one.

Useful links

The original article on OECD Insights, including links and supplementary material, can be found here: *http://wp.me/p2v6oD-2D9*

The full series can be found here: *http://oecdinsights.org/?s=NAEC+complexity*

Development as the outcome of a complex adaptive system

by Frans Lammersen and Jorge Moreira da Silva (Director),
OECD Development Co-operation Directorate – DCD-DAC

In *The Wealth of Nations*, Adam Smith wrote that: "Little else is requisite to carry a state to the highest degree of opulence from the lowest barbarism but peace, easy taxes, and a tolerable administration of justice: all the rest being brought about by natural course of things." Others were less optimistic. They argued that nations are rich or poor because of differences in religion, culture, endowments, and/or geography.

Modern economic development theories originate from thinking about how to reconstruct Europe in the aftermath of World War II. The European Recovery Program – or the Marshall Plan – was based on the notion that economic growth can be stifled by local institutions and social attitudes, especially if these influence the domestic savings and investments rate. According to this linear growth model, a correctly-designed massive injection of capital coupled with public sector intervention to address market failures would ultimately lead to industrialisation and economic development. Many other economic development theories have since followed, but none have been able to explain convincingly why some countries experience rapid economic growth and others not.

The development community has continued its quest for the missing ingredient to ignite economic growth. Candidates have included capital, technology, policies, institutions, better politics, and market integration. Every time we think we have identified what's missing, we find that it is actually not something which can be provided from outside, but turns out to be an endogenous characteristic of the system itself. Traditionally, development assistance has been rooted in a type of engineering, mass production, conveyor belt mentality, with agencies promoting "silver bullet" solutions for such complex problems as eradicating malaria, reducing vulnerability, improving resilience, strengthening connectivity etc. Unfortunately, piecemeal or one step at a time development programmes often failed to deliver.

Increasingly, complexity thinking – a way of understanding how elements of systems interact and change over time – has found its way into the development discourse. After all, what could be more complex than promoting development, sustainability, human rights, peace, and governance? We should think of the economy and society as being composed of a rich set of interactions between large numbers of adaptive agents, all of which are coevolving. Based on this approach development is not just an increase in outputs, but the emergence of an interlinked system of economic, financial, legal, social and political institutions, firms, products and technologies. Together these elements and their interaction provide citizens with the capabilities to live happy, healthy and fulfilling lives.

Once we look at development as the outcome of a complex adaptive system instead of the sum of what happens to the people and firms, we will get better insights into how we can help accelerate and shape development. We would be more effective if we assess development challenges through this prism of complex adaptive systems. This could yield important insights about how best to prioritise, design and deliver holistic development programmes for achieving the multiple goals of inclusiveness, sustainability and economic growth that underpin the 2030 Sustainable Development Agenda. There is increasing support in aid agencies for the idea that solutions to complex problems must evolve, through trial and error – and that successful programmes are likely to be different for *each local context*, with its particular history, natural resources and webs of social relations. The key for anyone engaged in the aid business is to put their own preconceived ideas aside and first observe, map, and listen carefully to identify the areas where change for the better is already happening and then try to encourage and nurture that change further.

Complexity matters particularly when the knowledge and capacities required for tackling problems are spread across actors without strong, formalised institutional links. Inherent to many complex problems are divergent interests, conflicting goals or competing narratives. Moreover, it is often unclear how to achieve a given objective in a specific context, or change processes that involve significant, unpredictable forces. At the same time, it is important to emphasise that the counsel of complexity should not be taken as a counsel of despair for development. There has been immense social and economic progress, and development assistance has found to be helpful overall. Development co-operation has contributed to achieving economic objectives by helping developing countries connect their firms to international markets; to achieving social objectives by making globalisation pro-poor and reducing inequalities; and to environmental objectives by adapting to climate change while exploiting comparative advantages.

Not all development challenges are inherently complex though. For those that are, complexity should not be used as an excuse for fatalism and inertia. Instead we should strive to promote innovation, experimentation and renewal. We should build partnerships to learn about the past, allowing us to shape approaches that are more likely to work and that are owned by the people we are trying to help. They will tell us what is working and what is not. Together we should build a narrative for change involving many different voices and perspectives. We should also be modest and realise that it might better to start small and learn and adapt as we go along in iterative processes of dialogue. We should keep looking for change, scanning widely for new factors emerging in the wider world; listen to a wide range of opinions to be better able to anticipate and adapt and seize opportunities.

Embracing complexity where it matters will allow us to contribute more effectively to the 2030 Sustainable Development Agenda.

Useful links

The original article on OECD Insights, including links and supplementary material, can be found here: *http://wp.me/p2v6oD-2ML*

The full series can be found here: *http://oecdinsights.org/?s=NAEC+complexity*

Towards a new narrative

Sing for our time too, or what Homer can teach us about complexity

by Patrick Love, OECD Public Affairs and Communications Directorate

The September 2016 Workshop on Complexity and Policy organised by the OECD New Approaches to Economic Challenges (NAEC) team along with the European Commission and the Institute for New Economic Thinking (INET) included a discussion about how you build a narrative around complexity. As one participant pointed out, "complexity economics" isn't the most thrilling of titles, except (maybe) to complexity economists. But "narrative" was one of the keywords of the discussions, along with "navigating" complexity. If you add to this Lex Hoogduin's plea for modesty in his article on Insights and during the debate, I think we could learn something from an expert on narrative, navigation, and modesty: Homer.

The *Iliad* and *Odyssey* start with similar requests to the Muse to tell the tale of the hero, but with one striking exception. In *The Iliad*, she is asked to tell of the anger of Achilles, and the epic that follows is a more or less chronological account of ten days at the end of the Trojan War. In *The Odyssey* on the other hand, the poet suggests that the goddess start the tale wherever she thinks is best. One reason could be that, in our terms, *The Iliad* is a linear account, where one event causes and leads to the next, while *The Odyssey* is complex, jumping all over the place in space and time, with events far apart influencing each other, often in unintended ways.

Where you start a complex narrative determines what you describe and to some extent how you describe it. If, for example, you start your explanation of the financial crisis with the collapse of Lehmann Brothers, you will tell the story one way. If you start a few years earlier with market deregulation, the story will be different. Go back to the end of unlimited liability of stakeholders and yet another plot and set of characters become possible. Wherever you started, you would tell the true story, but not the only story. So in telling a complex story, you have to first decide what you want the audience to remember, and then decide what combination of the limitless elements available would best allow them to understand the issues and agree with a course of action.

Another lesson we can learn from Homer is that in a non-complex telling, there can be a "God's-eye view" of the narrative, as when Achilles contemplates the shield made for him by the god Hephaestus. In The Odyssey, the narrator doesn't have this knowledge, and is in fact part of the story himself, influencing its outcome. Eric Beinhocker of INET, who co-organised the NAEC Complexity workshop, relates this to Gödel's incompleteness theorems, arguing that it may be impossible for an agent embodied within the system to access information an agent outside the system with a God's-eye view would have.

Once you have decided what you want to say and selected what you are going to use to say it, there remains the question of how to say it. Policy experts, like experts in other fields, often defend their poor communication by explaining that the subject is complicated and shouldn't be dumbed down. Here's an extract from Einstein's critique of Newtonian cosmology in Relativity: The Special and General Theory: "If we ponder over the question as to how the universe, considered as a whole, is to be regarded, the first answer that suggests itself to us is surely this: As regards space (and time) the universe is infinite. There are stars everywhere, so that the density of matter, although very variable in detail, is nevertheless on the average everywhere the same. In other words: However far we might travel through space, we should find everywhere an attenuated swarm of fixed stars of approximately the same kind and density."

Practically any adult or young person who can read can understand Einstein's point, however complicated the subject. Here by way of contrast is the OECD explaining a fundamental concept in economics: "…the relative cost differences that define comparative advantage, and are the source of trade, disappear once one reaches equilibrium with free trade. That is, the two countries in the trading equilibrium in Figure 1.2 are both operating at points on their PPFs where the slope is equal to the common world relative price. Thus comparative advantage cannot be observed, in a free trade equilibrium, from relative marginal costs." Can you tell from this if we're for or against free trade?

It's striking that in so many domains, the greatest experts are the greatest advocates for simplicity. David Hilbert set the agenda for 20th century mathematics at the 1900 International Congress of Mathematicians in Paris in a paper on 23 unsolved problems. Hilbert supported the view that: "A mathematical theory is not to be considered complete until you have made it so clear that you can explain it to the first man whom you meet on the street". Maths genius Alan Turing was even more provocative, claiming that "No mathematical method can be useful for any problem if it involves much calculation." (Turing wrote a paper on computability without using any equations, basing his explanation on puzzles sold in toyshops.)

We can learn a final lesson from Homer in the character of his heroes. Achilles is arrogant, immature, impulsive, self-centred ("the best of the Achaeans", making you wonder what the rest of them were like). He's strong and is good at killing people but ends up dead. Ulysses is clever and is good at persuading people. He is modest and he listens to advice. He worries about others. And he navigates his way back to Ithaca and Penelope. In a complex world, today or as described by Homer, you will achieve more through strategy and resourcefulness than by brute force. The poet doesn't just ask the goddess to "start from where you will", he asks her to "sing for our time too".

Useful links

The original article on OECD Insights, including links and supplementary material, can be found here: *http://wp.me/p2v6oD-2Ed*

The full series can be found here: *http://oecdinsights.org/?s=NAEC+complexity*

A new narrative for a complex age

by Eric Beinhocker, Executive Director, The Institute for New Economic Thinking at the Oxford Martin School

If 2008 was the year of the financial crash, 2016 was the year of the political crash. In that year we witnessed the collapse of the last of the four major economic-political ideologies that dominated the 20th century: nationalism; Keynesian pragmatism; socialism; and neoliberalism. In the 1970s and 80s the centre right in many countries abandoned Keynesianism and adopted neoliberalism. In the 1980s and 90s the centre left followed, largely abandoning democratic socialism and adopting a softer version of neoliberalism.

For a few decades we thought the end of history had arrived and political battles in most OECD countries were between centre-right and centre-left parties arguing in a narrow political spectrum, but largely agreeing on issues such as free trade, the benefits of immigration, the need for flexible efficient markets, and the positive role of global finance. This consensus was reinforced by international institutions such as the IMF, World Bank, and OECD, and the Davos political and business elite.

In 2008 that consensus was rocked, last year it crumbled. Some will cling on to the idea that the consensus can be revived. They will say we just need to defend it more vigorously, the facts will eventually prevail, the populist wave is exaggerated, it's really just about immigration, Brexit will be a compromise, Clinton won more votes than Trump, and so on. But this is wishful thinking. Large swathes of the electorate have lost faith in the neoliberal consensus, the political parties that backed it, and the institutions that promoted it. This has created an ideological vacuum being filled by bad old ideas, most notably a revival of nationalism in the US and a number of European countries, as well as a revival of the hard socialist left in some countries.

History tells us that populist waves can lead to disaster or to reform. Disaster is certainly a realistic scenario now with potential for an unravelling of international co-operation, geopolitical conflict, and very bad economic policy. But we can also look back in history and see how, for example, in the US at the beginning of the 20th century Teddy Roosevelt harnessed populist discontent to create a period of major reform and progress.

So how might we tilt the odds from disaster to reform? First, listen. The populist movements do contain some racists, xenophobes, genuinely crazy people, and others whom we should absolutely condemn. But they also contain many normal people who are fed up with a system that doesn't work for them. People who have seen their living standards stagnate or decline, who live precarious lives one paycheque at a time, who think their children will do worse than they have. And their issues aren't just economic, they are also social and psychological. They have lost dignity and respect, and crave a sense of identity and belonging.

They feel – rightly or wrongly – that they played by the rules, but others in society haven't, and those others have been rewarded. They also feel that their political leaders and institutions are profoundly out of touch, untrustworthy, and self-serving. And finally they feel at the mercy of big impersonal forces – globalisation, technology change, rootless banks and large faceless corporations. The most effective populist slogan has been "take back control".

After we listen we then have to give new answers. New narratives and policies about how people's lives can be made better and more secure, how they can fairly share in their nation's prosperity, how they can have more control over their lives, how they can live with dignity and respect, how everyone will play by the same rules and the social contract will be restored, how openness and international co-operation benefits them not just an elite, and how governments, corporations and banks will serve their interests, and not the other way around.

This is why we need new economic thinking. This is why the NAEC initiative is so important. The OECD has been taking economic inequality and stagnation seriously for longer than most, and has some of the best data and analysis of these issues around. It has done leading work on alternative metrics other than GDP to give insight into how people are really doing, on well-being. It is working hard to articulate new models of growth that are inclusive and environmentally sustainable. It has leading initiatives on education, health, cities, productivity, trade, and numerous other topics that are critical to a new narrative.

But there are gaps too. Rational economic models are of little help on these issues, and a deeper understanding of psychology, sociology, political science, anthropology, and history is required. Likewise, communications is critical – thick reports are important for government ministries, but stories, narratives, visuals, and memes are needed to shift the media and public thinking.

So what might such a new narrative look like? My hope is that even in this post-truth age it will be based on the best facts and science available. I believe it will contain four stories:

➤ A new story of growth.

➤ A new story of inclusion.

➤ A new social contract.

➤ A new idealism.

This last point doesn't get discussed enough. Periods of progress are usually characterised by idealism, common projects we can all aspire to. Populism is a zero-sum mentality – the populist leader will help me get more of a fixed pie. Idealism is a positive-sum mentality – we can do great things together. Idealism is the most powerful antidote to populism.

Economics has painted itself as a detached amoral science, but humans are moral creatures. We must bring morality back into the centre of economics in order for people to relate to and trust it. Some might question whether this is territory the OECD should get into. But the OECD was founded "to improve the economic and social well-being of people around the world" and provide a forum for governments to "seek solutions to common problems." These issues will dramatically impact the well-being of people around the world for decades to come and are certainly a common problem.

So my hope is that the OECD will continue to play a leadership role, through NAEC and its other initiatives, on new economic thinking, not just in a narrow technical sense, but in the broad sense of helping forge a new vision that puts people back at the centre of our economy. We are truly at a fluid point in history. It could be a great step backwards or a great step forwards. We must all push forwards together.

Useful links

The original article on OECD Insights, including links and supplementary material, can be found here: *http://wp.me/p2v6oD-2Nl*

The full series can be found here: *http://oecdinsights.org/?s=NAEC+complexity*

Telling the whole truth in a post-truth environment

by Gabriela Ramos, OECD Chief of Staff and Sherpa to the G20

In 2016, surprisingly for many, Oxford Dictionaries chose as their Word of the Year "post-truth", an adjective defined as: *"relating to or denoting circumstances in which objective facts are less influential in shaping public opinion than appeals to emotion and personal belief"*. This runs contrary to the main tenet of the OECD, the "house of best practices" whose works and analysis depend on high quality statistics and solid empirical evidence. So how did we get here, and what does it means for our democracies?

As the OECD's G20 Sherpa, I witnessed the evolution of what was originally a financial crisis into an economic crisis, and more recently, after eight years of low growth and very slow recovery, into a political crisis defined by the lack of trust of people in the institutions that we built over so many decades. It is also clear that the values of openness, mutual assistance, and international integration on which the OECD was founded are being questioned.

One reason for this is that while we have told "the truth and nothing but the truth", we have not told "the whole truth". Like people gradually enclosing themselves in media silos and social networks that only give them news and views they are comfortable with, we have been happy to rely on economic models that work with comfortingly quantitative facts on GDP, income per capita, trade flows, resource allocation, productivity, and the like. These standard economic models did not anticipate the level of discontent that was created by the skewed outcomes that they were delivering, and that have prevailed for so many years.

Our "truths" did not capture very relevant dimensions that inform people's decisions (including recent political decisions), and particularly those that are intangible or non-measurable concepts. This is why such important issues as justice, trust or social cohesion were just ignored in the models. Indeed, neoliberal economics taught us that people are rational, and that they will always take the best decisions according to the information they have to maximise utility. And that accumulation of rational decisions will deliver the best outcome on the aggregates. In this model there is no room for emotions or for concepts like fairness or resentment.

Populism, the backlash against globalisation, call it what you will, recognises these emotions. We should do so too, especially since we actually have the data and facts that gave rise to these feelings in the first place. I am referring to the increased inequalities of income and outcomes that almost all the OECD economies experienced even before the crisis and that the crisis made worse.

If we go beyond averages and GDP per capita and look at the distributional impact of our economic decisions for instance, the picture is devastating. Up to 40% of people in the lowest tenth of the income distribution in OECD countries (and 60% in my own country, Mexico) have not seen their situation improve in the last decades. On top of that, lower income groups accumulate disadvantages, as their initial condition does not allow them to access quality education and health care or fulfilling jobs, while their children are facing a sombre future with less chance of improving their lot. At the OECD we have confirmed this. Our data show that if you are born into a family whose parents did not reach higher education, you have four times less chance of reaching middle school. You may encounter more health problems, and have less fulfilling jobs and lower wages. You are trapped in a vicious circle of deprivation.

Even the loosely-defined middle classes in OECD countries are fearful for their future and that of their children. They too feel betrayed and are angry that despite working hard, saving and doing everything else that was supposed to guarantee a good life, they see the fruits of success being captured by a tiny elite while they are left behind. No wonder they are attracted to solutions that resonate with their emotions and seem to give them some hope.

What should an organisation like the OECD, committed to evidence-based policy advice, do in this context? First, we must speak out when there is a deliberate misrepresentation of the facts and realities. Even if the people delivering these lies are not aware of it, it does not discharge them from the responsibility to check the evidence. Presenting a view that is based on lies by omission or on purpose should be recognised as such and not go unchallenged in the "post-truth" environment.

Second, instead of defending our selection of facts, recognise that they were also biased, and that in many instances they represented preconceived notions of how the economy functions that have been proven wrong. To rebuild trust in the facts we produce to explain social and economic phenomena, we must ensure that they really represent the whole reality and provide workable solutions. We may need to start, as the Chief Statistician of the OECD has said, "to measure what we treasure and not treasure what we measure".

Most of all we need to understand that economic challenges are not just economic. That is why the OECD's New Approaches to Economic Challenges (NAEC) initiative promotes a multi-dimensional view of people's well-being, with tangible and intangible elements (including emotions and perceptions) all worthy of consideration. The NAEC agenda is ambitious, calling for a new growth narrative that recognises the complexity of human behaviour and institutions, and calls on sociology, psychology, biology, history, and other disciplines to help write this narrative and build better models to inform economic decisions.

We thought there was only one truth, and we promoted it without considering that it may have had faults. We defined reality in certain ways and ignored critics to the models. We strongly, and mistakenly, believed markets were the whole answer.

I think that as economists and policy makers, we should remember that in *The Wealth of Nations*, Adam Smith was drawing conclusions from not just the methodology, but also the ethics and psychology he explored in *The Theory of Moral Sentiments*. We may need to enrich our models to ensure that the outcomes respond to people expectations, and help us to recover the most important ingredient in our societies, which is trust.

Useful links

The original article on OECD Insights, including links and supplementary material, can be found here: *http://wp.me/p2v6oD-2NH*

The full series can be found here: *http://oecdinsights.org/?s=NAEC+complexity*

OECD PUBLISHING, 2, rue André-Pascal, 75775 PARIS CEDEX 16
(01 2017 03 1 P) ISBN 978-92-64-27152-4 – 2017